An Affair of the Heart

To Our Lady of the Angels of the Portiuncula

In loving memory of my parents
Albert and Sheila Jordan

An Affair of the Heart

A Biblical and Franciscan Journey

Patricia Jordan, FSM

GRACEWING

First published in 2008

Gracewing
2 Southern Avenue
Leominster
Herefordshire HR6 0QF

ISBN 978 0 85244 690 4

Typeset by Action Publishing Technology Ltd,
Gloucester GL1 5SR
Printed in England by
Athenaeum Press Ltd,
Gateshead NE11 0PZ

Contents

Foreword

IN THE TESTAMENT OF St Francis we read, 'The Most High Himself made it clear to me that I must live the life of the Gospel.' St Francis' life was a spiritual journey in which he made the Gospel live in him. Closeness to the Word Incarnate through the written word of Scripture was at the centre of St Francis' daily life. In drawing out the evangelical counsels of poverty, chastity and obedience from the Gospels, St Francis established the basis for Religious Life for many Orders and Congregations, not just Franciscans. This is one of the ways that love of God is made real for the world.

Sister Patricia Jordan, by opening the pages of Holy Scripture for us, leads us into a deeper understanding of St Francis' love affair with God. The vocation of a religious is not for everyone but all are called to holiness, and this book will help many as they journey along that path in company of St Francis.

+Malcolm McMahon, OP
Bishop of Nottingham

Preface

I FIRST MET SISTER PATRICIA JORDAN when she came as a graduate student to the college where I was teaching. She was a specialist in Religious Education and chose to write her dissertation, which I supervised, on the prophet Hosea. Later she expanded it into a doctorate, which again I supervised. I was privileged to learn much from Sister Patricia's research.

When his wife deserted him, Hosea discovered the real significance of God's love. Far from wanting his wife punished, as was his legal right, Hosea realized that he wanted to forgive her and take her back. From this, Hosea realized that this is how God treats his people. God is faithful to his promises no matter how much his people betray him. His love is unconditional and steadfast. He is always ready to renew the covenant relationship.

This was the foundation of St Francis of Assisi's discovery of God's love and Francis' embracing of poverty. He laid himself open to God's steadfast love by ensuring that possessions would not stand in its way. Just as Jesus had been steadfast in his response to his Father's love, even if it meant crucifixion, so too St Francis was prepared to respond unreservedly to that same love. In the end God recognized his devotion by granting him the stigmata, the marks of crucifixion imprinted on his body.

I believe that many people, whether members of religious communities, priests or laity, will find this book interesting and spiritually inspiring. Unconditional love transformed St Francis' own life; this book is a challenge to open ourselves to the unconditional love of God and journey with St Francis on the road to transformation in Christ.

Dr Joseph Rhymer, B.A., M.Th.,Th.D.

Acknowledgements

THE FOUNDATION FOR THIS book is my Doctoral Thesis entitled *A Spirituality of the Heart in the Context of the Franciscan Eremitical Tradition*. Therefore, from the inception of this project I am deeply indebted to a great number of people for contributing to this venture of faith resulting in the thesis, two books and a new building, the Portiuncula, associated with it. Without the inspiration and empowerment of the Holy Spirit of God, and the prayer, help, encouragement, skill and expertise of so many people, the faith-filled vision could not have become the reality it is today.

Heartfelt gratitude and appreciation fall neatly into two parts: the written research and the practical implementation in the beautiful building of the Portiuncula. In both areas I am deeply grateful to Sister Columba, my Superior General, and my Congregation for supporting this venture throughout. My own community of Sisters here at St Clare's deserve a special 'Thank You' for their on-going prayer, support, help and encouragement. This truly has been a community and congregational adventure in faith.

To Dr Joseph Rhymer, friend and mentor. His unfailing encouragement from the very beginning of this project and his shared love of the living Word of God have sustained and supported me throughout. To him I owe a particular 'Thank you'.

To Fr Regis Armstrong, OFMCap., whose love of all things Franciscan inspired this journey of the heart. I am deeply indebted to him for his encouragement to pursue this line of discovery by delving more deeply into the heart of Francis and making it a living message for the twenty-first century.

To Fr Andre Cirino, OFM and to Fr Michael Higgins, OFM for leading our Sisters in Days and Weeks of Franciscan Solitude in a deepening understanding of the Franciscan call to the hermitage of the heart.

To Sr Elizabeth Mary Imler, OSF and to Sr Kathleen Anne Copp, OSF for facilitating forty Days of Franciscan Solitude in preparation for undertaking this written and building project.

To Sr Frances Teresa Dowling, OSC: her prayerful support, reading of the text and valuable suggestions were always deeply appreciated.

To Professor Van Wyk for sound advice and on-going support. To Peg and Byron Evans of the Greenwich School of Theology for their confidence in this project from the outset. Peg's proofreading and grammatical skills were always generously shared with infinite patience and the warmth of friendship.

To all those in Ireland, Scotland, Wales, France, Hungary and America who opened their homes and their hearts in sharing their experience of living the eremitical life.

Many other people have assisted in offering library facilities and translation expertise. I am deeply grateful and appreciative: to Fr Rufus, OCSO and Dom Ambrose, OCSO at Mount St Bernard Abbey, Leicestershire; to the Library Staff at the Franciscan Study Centre in Canterbury; to Francoise Boardman for time given to French translations; to Margaret O'Beirne for Italian translations; to Fr Ivo, OFM at the Antonianum in Rome and to Sr Maria, Sr Anthony, Sr Carol and Sr Shirley for countless hours of library assistance; to Sr Dorothy Paul for hours of sharing her computer expertise; to Sr Marianne and Anne Marie O'Flynn for valuable Internet and computer advice and assistance; to Sr Bonaventure for generously giving her time to drive me to the many places connected with this research both in its written and building expression; and to all my Sisters for giving me the time and opportunity to complete this book and project, I thank them from my heart.

The written research is expressed in the building of the Portiuncula. Special thanks are due to Dominic Williams from

Ellis-Williams Architects and to his design team, especially Marhami Arifin, Steve Fitch and Ralph Forder for their sensitive, skilful and empathetic interpretation of our vision for the Portiuncula.

Thanks go also to Bosco Construction, especially the Directors, Bruno Quiligotti and Paul Marsh, for accepting this contract with great confidence and optimism. We extend our special thanks and appreciation to Mike Murray and all those too numerous to mention, but all appreciated, who have worked with him on site.

To Bowmer and Kirkland Property Services Limited for their dedicated undertaking of the Completion Works. Special thanks go to Peter Hawkins and his team for their competence, co-operation and sensitivity in making our vision a reality. To Jon and his team of workers on site, again too numerous to mention, our heartfelt thanks and prayerful appreciation.

To Alan Arnott of Studio Nine for Lighting; to Scobie Alvis of Faber Maunsell for Structural Engineering; to David Hibbert and Richard Trench of Goth Hibbert for Quantity Surveying; to Cate Watkinson for her original and inspirational interpretation of the Canticle of St Francis in stained glass; to Ram Roof for supplying a beautiful and ecologically friendly 'Green Roof'; to Real Stone for their donation of a stone fountain and their expertise in creating a real 'hermitage' expression, modelled on the Portiuncula hermitage in Assisi: thank you to them all.

I wish to express my deep gratitude to Tom Longford from Gracewing Publishing and to Sr Mary Joseph, OSB for her very gentle and patient working with me through the manuscript to bring the text to its present book form.

To so many people, named and unnamed, I commend each and all to the heart of God in deep gratitude and appreciation.

Finally, I am grateful to the owners of copyright material for their permission to reproduce extracts from the following: *The Catechism of the Catholic Church* and Nan C. Merrill, *Psalms for Praying*, The Continuum International Publishing Group Ltd; *Francis of Assisi*, *Early Documents*, vols I–III, New City; *The Jerusalem Bible*, Darton, Longman & Todd Ltd.

Introduction

THE LOVE OF GOD and the mystery of the human heart have captured my attention for many years. A particular focus began to emerge during my First Degree studies in Divinity when an enthusiastic Scripture scholar, Dr Joseph Rhymer, opened the Scriptures to his students in a way that I had not experienced before. Perhaps it just happened to be the right moment for me to hear the great love story of the Bible. It was the Hebrew word *hesed*[1] that opened new and exciting avenues of discovery and experience. Once begun, there was no turning back. The tender, steadfast love of God, revealed in Scripture as *hesed*, thrilled my being with wonder and awe and with fascination and feeling to such an extent that I lived it, breathed it and yearned to enter more deeply into its mystery.

Later came the opportunity to complete a Master's Degree in Franciscan Studies. St Francis, in his realization and experience of the extravagant love of God in Christ, especially when it is not reciprocated by those on whom it is lavished, cried out: 'Love is not loved.' I resonated with this cry especially as I wrestled with St Bonaventure's mystical writing: *The Soul's Journey into God*. Under the scholarly expertise of Regis Armstrong, OFM Cap., the Life and Writings of St Francis and St Clare came alive with an originality and freshness I had only glimpsed before. Father Regis paid particular attention to 'the landscape of the heart and its whereabouts'.[2] This led me to a deeper exploration of the meaning of the word 'heart' in both the Bible and in the writings of St Francis.

From the agony of his prayer for enlightenment of heart before the San Damiano Crucifix to the ecstasy of his Calvary experience on La Verna, the journey of St Francis into his own heart penetrated regions calling for exploration within my own. I was on fire yet again with the mystery of the human heart and the love that drives and energizes the search.

Through my own faith journey and in sharing the journeys of others, especially in the ministry of teaching and formation, captivation with the mystery of love and the mystery of the human heart led me to pursue doctoral studies culminating with a PhD thesis focusing on *A Spirituality of the Heart in the Context of the Franciscan Eremitical Tradition.* I paid particular attention to the part the desert or hermitage experience plays in the heart's formation and transformation. This led to new insights, new experiences, new challenges and a new 'place' both literally and symbolically. The journey of the heart is a life-long adventure and just when we think we have 'arrived' we are invited or challenged to set out again. It is always new.

The discovery of the richness and depth of *hesed*, heart and hermitage and the inter-relatedness of all three, is the context of our present reflections. The place of the desert-hermitage (I use desert and hermitage interchangeably) in our relationship with God is pivotal. Those haunting words from the prophet Hosea are of special significance:

> I am going to seduce her and lead her into the desert
> and speak to her heart.
> I shall betroth you to myself for ever,
> I shall betroth you in uprightness and justice,
> and faithful love and tenderness [*hesed*].
> Yes, I shall betroth you to myself in loyalty
> and in the knowledge of Yahweh. (Hos. 2:16, 21–22)

Hesed, heart and hermitage: these are the three areas explored in this book in the context of a journey, discovering 'the breadth and the length, the height and the depth; so that knowing the love of Christ, which is beyond knowledge, we may be filled with the utter fullness of God' (Eph. 3:19).

Like any love affair, it is first of all the passion and power of love that attracts, consumes and gives energy for the journey.

There is a youthful freshness, a lively sense of adventure and an intense desire to continue the search for the union of love and intimacy. Gradually, love reveals that all is not what it seems. When the honeymoon is over, the real challenges have to be faced, and then the desert experience reveals its other face: purification.

Intimacy and union are costly. Purification and conversion have many faces according to the life circumstances and personal vocation of every individual. I cannot tell you the very personal details of your heart's journey, but what I can tell you is that you are always loved. From eternity to eternity, you are always loved and perhaps the only way to enter the depths of this truth is to spend some time in the desert where the secret of solitude[3] will set your heart on fire in a way that has yet to be revealed.

When the secret of solitude is revealed to you within your own personal vocation and life circumstances, then you too will be fired with a sense of mission in reaching out to the hearts of others. This is how it happened for me. First through my teaching and formation ministry which continues to this day, and then in bringing to birth a brand new purpose-built House of Franciscan Prayer and Solitude to assist others on their heart's journey to experience the reality of being always loved.

Being encouraged by others to write about the Portiuncula and the heart's journey, I offer these reflections as an act of love, praying that as you delve deeper into your own heart, you will continue to discover there the heart of God dwelling within you as he promised he would:

> Anyone who loves me will keep my word,
> and my Father will love him,
> and we shall come to him
> and make a home in him. (Jn. 14:23)

Chapter 1 will take you into the Word of God where some of the richness and depth of the divine *hesed* are revealed. This love is passionate, personal, unconditional and all-embracing, desiring and inviting a personal and loving response. To do this requires setting aside a time and a place that we will refer to as your own 'desert' or place of solitude, in this book referred to as hermitage. Creating an atmosphere where you can be silent and attentive to the word within you is part of the adventure and lure of the hermitage experience. The emphasis is first and foremost on intimacy and union.

Having heard the word and responded to it in the experience and conviction of being loved, Chapter 2 presents the divine *hesed* with a human face, the Word made flesh, Jesus Christ. In him we see fully how the call *of* love and the response *to* love is fleshed out in a limited, fragile, vulnerable, fully human and beautiful life. The wonder of the revelation of the heart of God in and through Jesus opens the door to the mystery of love within the Trinity. Amazingly, we are caught up in this great mystery of love as we live our seemingly very ordinary human lives.

Chapter 3 invites us to accept the invitation and the challenge to accept our beauty and our brokenness. Only in Jesus, the Word made flesh do we have the grace and the courage to accept unconditional love and at the same time to delve deeper and face the apparently unredeemed corners of our hearts where the real battle ensues! The ego-driven self continues to fight for centre stage in our lives, and in the desert-hermitage experience of love's consuming and purifying fires, the battle within the heart is played out.

Chapter 4 focuses on the secret of solitude. We explore some of the implications of the heart's journey and the desired intimacy towards which our hearts yearn. Not only do we discover the landscape of our own hearts but we are led ever more deeply into the heart of our Trinitarian God where all our relationships are held in the embrace of God. Finally in Chapter 5, if we have persevered in the process of maturing in love, our heart's desire is at one with our response to surrender to love, totally and forever: love in return for Love.

In the companion to this volume, you are invited to *Come Apart and Rest for a While* in the company of St Francis and St Clare. Although the invitation is set within the new building, the Portiuncula in rural Derbyshire, England, the experience is not limited to a single place. The real hermitage is the heart and as St Francis reminds us: 'Brother Body is our cell, and our soul is the hermit who dwells within it, to pray to God and to meditate. If the soul does not live in peace and solitude in its cell, a cell made by hands profits a religious little.'[4]

Notes

1. *Hesed*: Scholars are not agreed on the proper translation of *hesed*, because no one word adequately describes or translates the Hebrew understanding. It is very definitely linked to covenant-love, which is self-giving, unconditional, compassionate, merciful, active love reaching out to others.
2. Armstrong, *St. Francis of Assisi: Writings for a Gospel Life*, p. 32.
3. 'The Major Legend of St. Francis by St. Bonaventure', in Armstrong *et al.*, *Francis of Assisi*, vol. 2, p. 539.
4. 'The Assisi Compilation', in Armstrong *et al.*, *Francis of Assisi*, vol. 2, p. 215.

Chapter 1

The Divine *Hesed*

WE ARE ALWAYS LOVED. This is a bold statement that rings with the truth of the Gospel. We may doubt it, question it, challenge it, refute it, resist it or reject it, but it is still true. And it is true because God has revealed it to us and he continues to engage us in a heart-to-heart encounter that longs for this revelation to become real in our lives. To hear this Word involves a journey inward to the depths of our hearts, that place of mystery and paradox and freedom and grace. If this journey seems daunting, know that God is with us every step of the way, loving us into the fullness of his life and love. Repeatedly in the pages of Scripture, God says: I am with you. Believe it and let us open our hearts to the heart of God.

Beginning the heart's journey is first of all an exercise in awareness and this is why it is worth spending a little time reflecting on the word 'heart' and its symbolism. It touches our daily lives in art, music, poetry and prose. Great authors, artists, poets and musicians have always been aware of the heart's appeal and power. It is a word and symbol with tremendous potential for healing and wholeness. Saint and sinner, young and old, rich and poor all understand the language of the heart, which breaks through barriers and boundaries in every age, creed and culture.

The symbol of the heart

The word 'symbol' means to draw together. In the context of our reflections on the heart as a symbol, we are speaking of the power of the heart to draw together and within itself all our experiences, positive and negative. It is also the place where life's paradoxes and contradictions are held together. According to the psychiatrist and author, Gerald May, 'Symbols are not only helpful but absolutely necessary for human functioning.'[1] They help us to touch realities that lie deep within us but often we are not fully aware of them. In this sense the symbol has the power to awaken new insights and revelations, which in turn lead to communion and integration. It is an inner adventure with far-reaching consequences for those who journey into the mystery of their own hearts. How about you? How aware are you of the evocative power of the heart symbol in music, art, advertisements, greeting cards, objects, poetry, prose, and in sacred Scripture? What is your understanding of the heart as a vehicle of expression, revelation, communication and communion?

The heart of God

Scripture scholars tell us that the word 'heart' is one of the most important and most used words in the Old Testament. It is a word that makes God accessible and understandable in human terms in our relationship with him. Therefore, Scripture uses heart in a very broad sense to include all aspects of life and behaviour because heart refers to the very core of who we are as persons. It is the source of our emotions, our thinking and our choosing and from this inner source flows all that is both good and evil. This is the biblical understanding of the heart that we are exploring and proclaiming. Perhaps the heart and the affective life are associated in the modern mind with a more restricted interpretation than in the biblical usage. This biblical understanding will unfold throughout the book as we enter into its mystery.

Each chapter will invite you to ponder and continue your heart's journey in a gradual process of awareness, acceptance, choice, challenge and response. My focus (and yours) must first be on love. Love is the language of the heart — always bearing in mind the richness and depth of both heart and love in biblical terms. It is the language of God revealing and proclaiming his infinite, eternal, and personal love for every human person. When we speak of love, our particular emphasis throughout will be on the tender, steadfast, merciful love of God that is referred to in Scripture as *hesed*.

Hesed is a Hebrew word having a richness and depth impossible to adequately translate into English. As no one word is used consistently in translation, we best understand it by studying the many words that the Bible has used in translation. We highlight two words in particular that are most commonly used with *hesed*: faith and mercy. Faith signifies steadfastness, loyalty and dependability; mercy signifies a compassionate, tender love reaching out to others with a heart sensitive to human misery and suffering.

Hesed is intimately connected to covenant-love in Scripture and both lie at the heart of God's revelation of himself and his relationship with us. Throughout the Old Testament there is development and various levels of intensity in the way in which *hesed* is understood and expressed. In the New Testament, God's love and the New Covenant reach fulfilment in the Person of Jesus Christ.

The far-reaching consequences of *hesed* as a response to and a reflection of covenant-love meant that every aspect of a person's life and behaviour was affected by this relationship. It was an affair of the heart in the biblical understanding of 'heart' as the totality of the person. The effects and fruits depend entirely on the state of one's heart, therefore, heart and *hesed* are intimately related and the desert-hermitage experience brings both into sharper focus.

When we speak of *hesed* in relation to God it expresses his unconditional, gratuitous, benevolent, grace-filled, merciful, tender, self-giving, self-emptying, steadfast and enduring love for every person. The far-reaching consequences are briefly summed up as follows: 'This divine *hesed* calls for corresponding *hesed* among human beings, consisting of self-giving, loving trust, abandonment, deep affection, piety, a love in short which is a joyful submission to the will of God and an active charity towards others.'[2]

Understandably, Scripture scholars are not agreed on the proper translation of *hesed*.[3] What they do agree on is that *hesed* is very definitely linked to covenant-love, which is self-giving, unconditional, compassionate, merciful, active love reaching out to others.

Love has always been the Good News of the Gospel and every heart has to hear it anew. Today, as you read this, the message is for you. Listen to it. Ponder it. Welcome it. Respond to it in your own personal and inimitable way. How important it is for us to get in touch with our heart, this secret place of encounter, where our deepest longings are held in a unique, graced and mysterious relationship with God.

Graced and gratuitous, let us marvel at God's choice of each one of us and let this be the foundation for our reflection and for setting out on the heart's journey. Scripture tells us that God 'set his heart on you and chose you ... because he loved you' (Dt. 7:7–8). Please don't pass over these wonderful words quickly. Learn to listen. Just stay with God's words and let them resound in the depths of your heart. Repeat them several times during the day and be grateful. Each person has to hear the Word of God as a personal word, a word that penetrates and pierces the heart and calls forth a response that transforms and divinizes.[4] This is what happened to St Francis.

The heart of Francis

One winter morning in February 1208, St Francis heard the words of the Gospel not only with his ears but also with his heart, and it changed his life forever. He exclaimed, 'This is what I want, this is what I seek, this is what I desire with all my heart.'[5] These words of St Francis, spoken in the little church of the Portiuncula, echo down the centuries and stir in the heart of every follower of St Francis who embarks on the Gospel journey into the heart of God. Not only followers of St Francis, but also every person seeking their heart's desire, can resonate with these words when eventually the heart is awakened by a personal word from God. At this point it might be worth asking oneself: 'What is *my* heart's desire?' because without desire it is not possible to set out on the journey of the heart.

It is interesting that St Francis uses the word heart more than any other when he speaks or writes about his love affair with God in Christ. Heart is that sort of word. It seems to say it all. As the great theologian, Karl Rahner said: 'Heart is one of the words in

which man, knowing himself, expresses the mystery of his existence without solving that mystery.'[6] St Francis was no excep-
tion. He certainly expressed the mystery of his existence by his
life of love in relationship with God, in relationship with every
person whom he welcomed as brother and sister and in the
embrace of all of created reality. He put into practice the word
that was addressed to him. God had intervened. From that day
on, Francis accepted that God had spoken to him in his Word
inviting a response.

We cannot overestimate the significance of 'The Word' for
Francis. According to the international Franciscan scholar, Regis
Armstrong, 'What makes the Franciscan approach so unique is its
focus not on structure or activity, place or time, occupation or
status, but simply on the human heart where the Word dwells.'[7]
The human heart where the Word dwells! What an astonishing
reality and how important it is to nurture the soil of the heart into
which the word 'so gently falls'.[8]

The words 'love of God' deeply moved the heart of Francis.
We are told he could not hear 'the love of God' without a change
in himself. As soon as he heard 'the love of God' he was excited,
moved, and on fire, as if these words from the outside were
strumming the strings of his heart on the inside. St Francis said:
'The love of him who loved us greatly is greatly to be loved.'[9] But
this did not happen overnight for Francis, and it won't happen
overnight for you or me. Francis had to take steps, make decisions, come before God as he really was and then in faith accept
God in Jesus, as the Way, the Truth and the Life. Yes, Jesus
became for Francis his way, his truth and his life.

St Francis had to learn to listen to the voice of God within his
heart and allow the Word to take root within him. This he did by
deliberately and attentively finding places of silence and solitude.
We are told that St Francis would seek a quiet place, a cave, a
hermitage, a broken-down church and there he struggled with the
question with which we all struggle: 'Who are You, Lord, and
who am I?' Often during those times apart, Francis experienced
God as father, brother, consoler, saviour, spouse and friend. You
are being invited to encounter God in the same way, and that is
why the hermitage experience is so important. Silence and soli-

tude have always been recognized as the favoured setting for hearing the truth of God's amazing love.

The heart and the hermitage

> But look, I am going to seduce her
> and lead her into the desert
> and speak to her heart.
> I shall betroth you to myself for ever,
> I shall betroth you in uprightness and justice,
> and faithful love and tenderness.
> Yes, I shall betroth you to myself in loyalty
> and in the knowledge of Yahweh. (Hos. 2:16, 21–22)

These words of Scripture are the words of a lover to his beloved. You are the beloved of God and these words are meant for you, today, as God reveals his heart to you. Karl Rahner states: 'Only the lover is able to pronounce the word "heart" with understanding.'[10] Give God permission to lead you to the desert-hermitage of your heart and there speak his word of love to you. The desert image is deliberately used because it is an image that is a familiar one in both sacred and secular poetry and prose. Let us linger a little on this image of the desert

The desert is the place of total exposure. There are no hiding places! It is a place of change and transformation. Whether real or symbolic it usually brings a person face to face with both the negative and positive within the human heart. It probably will not be easy at first to be there and wait upon God. Neither is it easy to really believe the truth about God's lavish, passionate, personal and unconditional love. Perhaps faith in the *hesed* of God enables and empowers us to venture into the desert-hermitage where we face the awesome reality of God's love.

Being attentive, receptive and responsive to God's word of love requires deep silence. It is indispensable in the heart-to-heart encounter within the solitude of the hermitage. Writing about the place of silence in the heart's journey, Henri Nouwen states that silence is the way to make solitude a reality and in so doing it completes and intensifies solitude.[11]

> Silence is the home of the word. Silence gives strength and fruit-
> fulness to the word. We can even say that words are meant to
> disclose the mystery of the silence from which they come ... If a
> word is to bear fruit it must be spoken from the future world into
> the present world.[12]

If it helps, just keep reading and repeating the promise of God in
his word to you, because God is faithful to his promises. In silence
let the words of Scripture sink into the soil of your heart and take
root there. In time they will grow and blossom even though you
may not be aware that it is so. What matters is that you desire to
accept this truth and allow it to transform your life. The Word of
God is that powerful because as Scripture says: 'The word of God
is something alive and active' (Heb. 4:12). May you experience
that inner life and activity as you open yourself to the fire of
God's love in the silence of your heart.

At this stage of your heart's journey, simply let yourself be
loved. This sounds easy but it is not. We may not feel very
lovable right now or we may feel unworthy of being loved. We
may also be aware that true love is costly. To love and to be loved
has consequences and I think most of us know this in the depths
of our hearts. Perhaps that is why we may even shy away from
real love.

Hesed, heart and hermitage: this is our focus and challenge for
a fully human life of love and the journey it entails. To love
means that we become vulnerable. To love means that we take
risks. To love means that we trust completely. To love means
that we step out in faith. To love means that we abandon
ourselves joyfully to the will of God. To love means giving
ourselves to Another and to others. This is the reality of *hesed*.
This is what the hermitage will teach you. This is the place where
your heart meets the heart of God, especially a God who became
poor to enrich you, a God who humbled himself to raise you up,
a God who patiently suffered to heal your wounds and unite you
to himself forever.

With St Paul we pray: 'Glory be to him whose power, working
in us, can do infinitely more than we can ask or imagine; glory be
to him from generation to generation in the Church and in Christ
Jesus for ever and ever. Amen' (Eph. 3:21).

God loves us always. Even when we forget or are indifferent, God continues to love passionately, personally, unconditionally and forever. We cannot change that reality. We are his heart's delight whether we accept it or not. Did he not say, 'My delight is in her. As the bridegroom rejoices in his bride, so will your God rejoice over you' (Is. 62:4–6). Sooner or later you too, like the Bride in the Song of Songs will emerge from your desert-hermitage, leaning on your Beloved and 'When that day comes – declares Yahweh – she will call me "My Husband"' (Hos. 2:16–18).

Whether we rest in God's love as the beloved of the bride-groom or as a child in its mother's arms, the call is to love, intimacy, trust and confidence. God himself tells us of his parental love and care:

> When Israel was a child I loved him. I myself taught Ephraim to walk, I myself took them by the arm, but they did not know that I was the one caring for them, that I was leading them with human ties, with leading-strings of love, that with them, I was like someone lifting an infant to his cheek, and that I bent down to feed him. (Hos. 11:1,3–4)

God bending down to us! Stay with this image if you can because this is the God of St Francis – a God who bends down to us in love to draw us to himself.

In pleading tones, we read in the prophet Isaiah: 'Can a woman forget her baby at the breast, feel no pity for the child she has borne? Even if these were to forget, I shall not forget you. Look, I have engraved you on the palms of my hands' (Is. 49:15–16). Such love! No wonder the Psalmist could say, 'I hold myself in quiet and silence, like a little child in its mother's arms, like a little child, so I keep myself' (Ps. 131:2–3). Yes, this is a wonderful image of love but it takes courage and confidence to be that little child before God. Ultimately, it means receiving God's love, not earning it or meriting it, but simply receiving it. Can you do that? If not, why not?

Our hearts

It is comforting for us to hear the Psalmist say that 'God alone knows the secrets of the heart' (Ps. 44:21). In the biblical understanding, the heart holds all our feelings, memories, ideas, plans, choices and desires. It is the centre of human life in all its dimensions. As we have already noted, great authors, artists and musicians seem to grapple with the way in which the heart reveals the totality of the person. In one of his novels, Charles Dickens refers to a person's features as 'the index of the heart', and the great Shakespeare in *The Winter's Tale* has Polixenes say: 'I saw his heart in his face.' Scripture too reminds us: 'A person's heart moulds his expression whether for better or worse' (Eccles. 13:25). Perhaps you are now beginning to see the centrality and importance of the heart both literally and symbolically. Our physical heart is hidden from view yet it is the life-giving force within the body; symbolically the heart is the life-giving centre of our personhood and call to love. If this is how you understand the heart then you are open to the mystery of existence.

In the Book of Proverbs we read: 'My child, if you take my words to heart ... turning your ear to wisdom, turning your heart to understanding ... you will understand and discover the knowledge of God' (Prov. 2:1–5). Here we are challenged to take the Word of God seriously and we may have to ask ourselves: Have we taken God's words to heart, really? In turning our ear to wisdom and our heart to understanding, we will discover that God has set his heart on each one personally and chosen us because he loves us. God loves you and me as individuals, as unique expressions of himself. He knows and calls us by name and we are precious and honoured in his sight. Yes, I know some of you who are reading these words have heard them many times before. Perhaps now is the time to take God at his word in a way you have never done before. Take his words to heart – to your heart.

Many people believe they must earn or deserve God's love. The reality of being always loved unconditionally is difficult for some people to accept. The truth is that we were loved into existence and our destiny is to love and be loved for all eternity. 'You created my inmost self, knit me together in my mother's womb.

For so many marvels I thank you; a wonder am I, and all your works are wonders' (Ps. 139:13–14). If you feel you wish to pause right now and make this prayer your own, then please do so. Love is the meaning and purpose of our lives and each of us must search for our personal vocation through which this call is expressed.

Even before Love assumed a human face and became flesh in the Person of Jesus Christ, God inundated us with protestations of his love for us. He did this through ordinary human channels, images and symbols that we would understand: marriage, parenthood and friendship. These images are among the most ordinary human experiences through which God reveals his love for us. In this chapter we have gathered some of the fragrant words of the Lord that reveal his precious and extravagant love.

Over the years I have copied God's words of love into my Prayer Journal where I reflect on them and cherish them as a personal word of love. I have savoured every *hesed* reference there is in sacred Scripture and I continue to wonder at the extravagance of God's love. Now, with Mary, the Mother of God, who pondered and treasured God's word in the silence of her heart, you are invited to ponder and treasure God's words of love to you in the depths and silence of your own heart.

The following words of love may be a starting point or a stepping-stone for your prayer and reflection. These words of love come to you from the silence of God: receive them into the silence of your heart and bring them to birth in the fruitfulness of your life. These in turn may lead you to explore in greater depth and intensity the many sacred texts revealing the divine *hesed* in the heart of God. Most of all the divine *hesed* is revealed to us in the human face of Jesus Christ and in his living among us as poor, humble and patiently suffering the pain of the human condition. This will be our focus in Chapter 2.

Invitations to Prayer

Words of Love
1. As a mother comforts her child, so I will comfort you. (Is. 66:13)

 2. I remember your faithful love, the affection of your bridal days. (Jer. 2:2)
 3. Look, I am doing something new. (Is. 43:19)
 4. Do not be afraid, for I have redeemed you; I have called you by name, you are mine. (Is. 43:1–2)
 5. I regard you as precious, you are honoured and I love you. (Is. 43:4)
 6. How beautiful you are, my love, and how you delight me! (Sg. 1:16)
 7. For I, Yahweh, your God, I grasp you by your right hand; I tell you: Do not be afraid, I shall help you. (Is. 41:14)
 8. Those who hope in me will not be disappointed. (Is. 49:23)
 9. For the mountains may depart, the hills be shaken, but my faithful love will never leave you. (Is. 54:10)
10. I have loved you with an everlasting love and so I still maintain my faithful love for you. (Jer. 31:3)
11. I have created you for my glory. (Is. 43:7)
12. Have no fear, do not be disheartened by anything. (Deut. 31:8)

Heart Reflections
 1. When you spend time praying and reflecting on the word/symbol 'heart', what emotions rise most readily from within?
 2. Compose your own prayer/poem/song for the qualities of heart you most desire.
 3. The poet Rilke said, 'Go and do heart work on all the images imprisoned within you.' What challenges do these words evoke in you?
 4. Spend some time with Jesus/Mary/Francis/Clare or one of your own favourite saints. Talk to them about their heart journey, especially during their desert-hermitage experiences. Ask them to walk with you and to teach you that you also may persevere in your own journey of the heart.

Psalm 113

Sing praises to the beloved
of all hearts!
Sing praises, all you who would
honour Love,
sing praises to the Creator of
the universe!
Bless the Holy One from this time forth
and forever more!
Aspire to know the Unknowable,
to enter fully into the
Great Mystery,
to be fertile ground to the
Heart-seed of Love.
Aspire to Gifts of the Spirit,
be open to Grace and express
gratitude!

Who is like the Blessed One,
the One who is Infinite Love,
Power, and Intelligence,
Who enters into human hearts
and brings comfort to those
in need?
Yes, those who call upon the
Merciful One,
are lifted up and blessed with
new life;
They wear a crown of joy,
as they recognize their
oneness with Spirit.
Come, all who suffer and are
heavy-laden,
open your hearts to Love!
Sing praises to the Heart of all hearts.

Psalm 139

O my Beloved, You have searched me
and known me!
You know when I sit down and
when I rise up;
You discern my innermost thoughts.
You find me on the journey and
guide my steps;
You know my strengths and
my weaknesses.
Even before words rise up in prayer,
Lo, You have already heard
my heart call.
You encompass me with love where'er
I go,
and your strength is my shield.
Such sensitivity is too wonderful
for me;
it is high; boundless gratitude
is my soul's response.

Where could I go from your Spirit?
or how could I flee from
your Presence?
If I ascend into heaven, You are there!
If I make my bed in darkness,
You are there!
If I soar on the wings of the morning
or dwell in the deepest parts
of the sea,
Even there your hand will lead me,
and your Love will embrace me.
If I say, 'Let only darkness cover me,
and the light about me be night',
Even the darkness is not dark to You,
the night dazzles as with the sun;
the darkness is as light with You.

For You formed my inward being,
You knit me together in my
mother's womb.

I praise You, for You are to be
reverenced and adored.
Your mysteries fill me with wonder!
More than I know myself do You know me;
My essence was not hidden from You,
when I was being formed in secret,
intricately fashioned from the
elements of the earth.
Your eyes beheld my unformed substance;
in your records were written
every one of them,
The days that were numbered for me,
when as yet there was none of them.
How precious to me are your creations,
O Blessed One!
How vast is the sum of them!
Who could count your innumerable
gifts and blessings?
At all times, You are with me.

O that You would vanquish my fears,
Beloved;
O that ignorance and suffering
would depart from me —
All that separates me from true
abandonment,
to surrendering myself into
your Hands!
Yet are these not the very thorns that
focus my thoughts upon You?
Will I always need reminders to
turn my face to You?
I yearn to come to You in love,
to learn of your mercy and wisdom!

Search me, O my Beloved, and know
my heart!
Try me and discern my thoughts!
Help me to face the darkness within me;
enlighten me, that I might
radiate your love and light![13]

Praying with St Francis

The Praises of God
You are holy, Lord God *Who* does wonderful things.
You are strong. *You are great*. You are most high.
You are the almighty king. You *holy* Father,
King of heaven and earth.

You are three and one, the Lord *God of gods*;
You are the good, all good, the highest good,
Lord God *living and true*.

You are love, charity; You are wisdom, You are humility,
You are patience, You are beauty, You are meekness,
You are security, You are rest,
You are gladness and joy, You are our hope, You are justice,
You are moderation, You are all our riches to sufficiency.

You are beauty, You are meekness.
You are the protector, You are our custodian and defender,
You are strength, You are refreshment. You are our hope,
You are our faith, You are our charity,
You are all our sweetness, You are our eternal life:
Great and wonderful Lord, Almighty God, Merciful Saviour.[14]

Notes
1. May, *Will and Spirit*, p. 111.
2. *The New Jerusalem Bible*, footnote u, p. 1501.
3. *The Jerusalem Bible* uses the following words as translations of the Hebrew word *hesed*: steadfast love; loving; loves; kind; kindness; grace; graciousness; tender (care); tenderness; mercy; merciful; favour; favours; goodness; pity; affection; pious deed; piety; goodwill; for my own good; gentleness; devout; beauty; generous; we will spare you; friendly; kindness and faithfulness.
4. Divinization is that mystery of participating in the life of Christ, in whose image we are created, accepted in faith as the fullness of our capacity as creatures, to share in the life of the Trinity.
5. 'The Life of Saint Francis by Thomas of Celano', in Armstrong *et al.*, *Francis of Assisi*, vol. 1, pp. 201–2.
6. Rahner, 'Heart', *Theological Investigations*, vol. 3, p. 323.
7. 'If My words remain in you', in Hammond (ed.), *Francis of Assisi*, p. 76.
8. Ibid., p. 75.

9. 'The Remembrance of the Desire of a Soul by Thomas of Celano', in Armstrong *et al.*, *Francis of Assisi*, vol. 2, p. 373.

10. Rahner, 'Heart', *Theological Investigations*, vol. 3, p. 321.

11. Nouwen, *The Way of the Heart*, p. 43.

12. Ibid., pp. 48–9.

13. Merrill, *Psalms For Praying*, pp. 241–2, 290–2.

14. 'The Praises of God,' in Armstrong *et al.*, *Francis of Assisi*, vol. 1, p. 109.

Chapter 2

Nearest the Father's Heart

GOD LOVES US. We have already explored some of the words of love revealed to us in sacred Scripture. Now we have the amazing revelation of God's love having a human face, a human heartbeat and a human name: Jesus, the Word made flesh, God living among us. This totally astonishing love in human form is the same eternal Son who was with God in the beginning (Jn. 1:1–2). St John goes on to tell us: 'No one has ever seen God; it is the only Son, who is nearest the Father's heart, who has made him known' (Jn. 1:18). God with a human face and a human heart! What amazing love! 'The Word became flesh, and he lived among us' (Jn. 1:14).

Speaking to his apostles in his Farewell Discourses, Jesus said: 'If you know me, you will know my Father too' (Jn. 14:6). Therefore, knowledge of the Father presupposes knowledge of Jesus. How well do you and I really know the Son who is nearest the Father's heart? We may have preconceived ideas about the Jesus of the Gospels. We may have scanty or abundant knowledge of the details of his life on earth. We may have true or false ideas about his teaching and the message of his earthly life among us. We may have doubts about his relevance for our daily lives. We may have created images of him according to our limited perceptions or favoured representations. Wherever we are in our relationship and knowledge of Jesus, we are invited to enter more deeply into the mystery by which we are already embraced.

If the Son is the only one who truly knows the Father, then let us ponder and pray for this heart-knowledge. Perhaps St Francis' Prayer for Enlightenment might be our starting point at this stage of the inner journey.

> Most High, glorious God,
> enlighten the darkness of my heart
> and give me
> true faith,
> certain hope,
> and perfect charity,
> sense and knowledge,
> Lord,
> that I may carry out
> Your holy and true command.[1]

The heart of God

God chose to be born at a particular time in history, in a particular place in history and within a particular family in history. We know the story well. Or do we? If we do, of what significance for us are the facts surrounding Jesus' birth and life circumstances, his public teaching, his death and resurrection? What do these truths reveal about the heart of God and his love for each one of us? How does Jesus reveal the heart of the Father? Let us prayerfully reflect on some of the revealed truths concerning God's coming among us in human flesh.

Knowing the Son who is nearest the Father's heart will be demanding and challenging for us. It was for those who knew him in Galilee and Jerusalem. Why? To some Jesus appeared to be too ordinary. These people knew his parents, his background, his relatives and his carpenter's bench. To others Jesus appeared too extraordinary. He made claims that were outlandish, even blasphemous! He claimed to forgive sin. He claimed equality with God. He claimed to give his flesh and blood to be eaten as the Bread of Life. He claimed to rise three days after death, thus overcoming death itself. He claimed to remain with us until the end of time. How well do we know Jesus? Let us dwell for a little while with the Jesus of the Gospels, our Way, our Truth and our Life, that we too may glimpse the heart of God beating in human flesh.

Let us begin at the beginning. 'In the beginning was the Word; the Word was with God and the Word was God. He was with God in the beginning. Through him all things came into being.'

And St John goes on to say: 'The Word became flesh and dwelt among us' (Jn. 1:1–2,14). What a stupendous revelation this is with such far-reaching consequences for every person and the whole of created reality.

In Jesus of Nazareth, born in a moment of time to a virgin named Mary, God entered our world in human form. The place of birth was a stable, the town was Bethlehem (meaning House of Bread) and the parents of the House of David had travelled from Nazareth, an obscure and relatively unimportant village in Palestine. This was how God chose to come among us! If we are not amazed by this truth, then perhaps we have not pondered, prayed and stayed with this mystery long enough.

God with a human heartbeat and a human face! The Word who was with God and is God from all eternity entered our created world in the womb of the Virgin Mary. Conceived by the power of the Holy Spirit and receiving his human nature from the humble and lowly Virgin of Nazareth, Jesus entered our world in the form of a tiny, helpless baby. Just like any other newborn baby, Jesus was needy, vulnerable, fragile and dependent. This is our God!

> Something which has existed from the beginning,
> which we have heard,
> which we have seen with our own eyes,
> which we have watched
> and touched with our own hands,
> the Word of life. (1 Jn. 1)

But what does the manner of his coming say to us? St Paul summed it up when he said:

> Make your own the mind of Christ Jesus:
> Who, being in the form of God,
> did not count equality with God
> something to be grasped. (Phil. 2:6)

From birth to death, the pattern of God's presence with us is most evident in the love that embraced poverty, humility and patient suffering. What else is this but identification with and participation in the human condition as it unfolds in a way that is familiar to each one of us? The Word was made flesh and lived among us. Johannes Metz says,

> We say this all too casually, because inadvertently we are accustomed to consider only the biological event, the external process. But the assumption of man's type of Being is primarily a spiritual venture pulsing through the free activity of our heart. It is an unfolding story, an inner journey.[2]

The unfolding story takes us deeply into the realm of the New Covenant brought to fulfilment in Jesus and manifesting the divine *hesed* through poverty, humility and patient suffering. During his preaching and teaching Jesus tried to form the hearts of his closest followers according to the heart of God. It was not easy for the apostles and it is not easy for us. At the heart of his life and teaching is the message of poverty and humility. Jesus asked his followers to learn from him that they too might become meek and humble in heart. On one occasion to illustrate his point in a very concrete and down to earth fashion, Jesus took a little child, put his arms around the child and taught the apostles to welcome the littleness, powerlessness and vulnerability the little child symbolized. Ironically, this lesson was given after the apostles had been disputing about power and greatness among themselves.

To walk the way of poverty, humility and patient suffering presents a perennial struggle for humanity. It is difficult to face up to and accept the limitations that are inherent in the human condition. Therefore power, pleasure and possessions hold a seductive fascination and attraction. Let us look briefly at the reality of each of these in the life of Jesus and the relevance of each in your life and mine, since Jesus manifests both the *hesed* of God and the desired human response to such extravagant love.[3]

The human face of God

Jesus, the One who is nearest the Father's heart and the image of the unseen God, came among us as the Word made flesh. In doing so, he has made it possible for everyone, everywhere, to live in a love relationship with God because he is both God and man. He whom St John describes as 'full of grace and truth' (Jn. 1:14) came to share life and love totally. 'Indeed, from his fullness we have, all of us, received – grace upon grace' (Jn. 1:16). Significantly, one of the many interpretations of *hesed* is grace. Jesus, full of the *hesed* of God, the steadfast, tender, merciful love of God, gifts us with the same grace. How aware are you of receiving grace upon grace from the heart of God?

Son of the Father from all eternity, Jesus did not cling to his equality with God but in a moment in history, through the Incarnation, he became as we are: poor. Here we are speaking not of material poverty but of intrinsic poverty, the fact that we are contingent beings, dependent on God for our very existence. Only the First-born, Jesus, can teach us how to become truly human. 'God, in giving us his Son, showed us what our existence is; he showed us the true nature of our humanness, and he showed us the proper spirit to have in becoming a human being: the spirit of poverty.'[4] The process of becoming is all-important. It was for Jesus and it is for us.

God *becomes* man. Jesus, the eternal Son of God becomes poor, powerless, dependent and defenceless in the human nature he assumed in the womb of the Virgin Mary. He was conceived by the power of the Holy Spirit and depended on the body of the Virgin Mary for growth and development as a human being. Here we also see the human *hesed* response of Mary to the divine *hesed* of God.

Mary of Nazareth gave herself totally, unconditionally and unreservedly to the will of God, in joyful submission and perfect trust and abandonment. In so doing, Mary enabled God's presence to become manifest and visible in human flesh and blood. What about us? Do we allow God to express his love and his life in us and through us in the Gospel of our everyday lives? Perhaps this is the moment to pause and ask Mary, mother of Jesus, and our mother to help us to bring Jesus to birth in our lives and in our world.

The Incarnation is the overwhelming revelation of the inner life of the Trinity – a community of Divine Persons in total self-giving, self-communicative, self-revealing, self-emptying love. In

Jesus, the mystery of the heart of God is made manifest. 'For this is how God loved the world: he gave his only Son' (Jn. 3:16). This is the poverty of God. The Father who is the Origin and the Giver of life and love, gives his only Son for our sakes. But how do we understand this statement: *For our sakes*?

Have you ever reflected on why Jesus came on earth and lived among us as a human being? Theologians have certainly pondered deeply and debated at length in finding an answer to this profound question and, throughout the history of the Church, they have presented differing views as to why God became man in Jesus Christ. For many people, salvation history follows the pattern of God creating the world and human beings. When human beings rebelled against God, a saviour was promised to redeem us and reconcile us with God. The saviour came as Jesus of Nazareth and he was crucified and died on the Cross for us. On the third day he rose from the dead, victorious over sin and death. This is true, of course, but there is a deeper question that we are asking, a question that has been asked since the Word became flesh and dwelt among us. The question is: If we had not sinned would the beloved Son have come among us as a human being?

You may be aware that during the Middle Ages the question as to why Christ came was debated by the great theologians of the time. Would Christ have come if humanity had not sinned? The Dominican theologian St Thomas Aquinas viewed the Incarnation as a remedy for sin. This view would make the Word made flesh, Jesus Christ, dependent on sin for his being among us. While recognizing the need for redemption, the Franciscan theologian, St John Duns Scotus held the view that sin was not the focus. He believed and taught that the divine love within the community of the Trinity was the reason for Christ's coming among us as a human being. Before the world was created, it was God's plan to share his life and love in and through the Word made flesh, Jesus Christ, the First-born of all creation.

The reflections in this book seek to present a biblical and Franciscan journey, emphasizing at the outset, that God sent his Son because of love, bringing us 'grace upon grace, gift upon gift' (Jn. 1:16). From all eternity God intended to dwell among us in the Incarnate Word, Jesus Christ, not because of sin but because of

love. The biblical foundation for this is in St John's Gospel and in
St Paul's Letters.

> In the beginning was the Word:
> The Word was with God
> And the Word was God.
> He was with God in the beginning.
> Through him all things came into being,
> not one thing came into being except through him. (Jn. 1:1–3)

Here we have the overflowing love of God embracing every
person and the whole of created reality in and through Jesus
Christ, the Word Incarnate. St Paul tells us that even before the
world was made, the Father chose us in Christ.

> Blessed be the God and Father of our Lord Jesus Christ,
> who has blessed us with all spiritual blessings of heaven in Christ.
> Thus he chose us in Christ before the world was made ...
>   (Eph. 1:3–4)

Throughout St John's Gospel the focus is *hesed* (the Greek equivalent is *agape*): a relationship of self-giving, sacrificial love, intimacy and indwelling, even *before* we rejected love and needed
redemption! Yes, the Incarnation does involve redemption but
sin is not the primary reason for the heart of God to beat in human
flesh. The primary reason is love, lavish and extravagant love that
wants to share itself and overflow into the whole of creation. As
Paul so aptly stated:

> He is the image of the unseen God,
> the first-born of all creation,
> for in him were created all things
> in heaven and on earth:
> everything visible and everything invisible,
> thrones, ruling forces, sovereignties, powers –
> all things were created through him and for him. (Col. 1:15–16)

This is our God: a God of love who gave his only Son to be the
First-born, the blueprint, and the centre of all created reality. In
him we live and move and have our being. The reason and

purpose for Jesus becoming human is to fulfil the eternal plan of God to share his life and love with us. And only the God-man Jesus could make a total response on behalf of us all and embracing us all. As the Franciscan scholar, Ilia Delio, states: 'When the Word became flesh, the eternal Word did not *leave* the Trinity to enter humanity; rather, the Word as eternal became incarnate. The capacity of the human person to be united to God, therefore, was fulfilled in the Incarnation.'[5] Only in Jesus can we see what *hesed* involves for both man and God thus revealing both the mystery of the heart of God and the mystery of our own hearts. Do you feel a sense of wonder, awe, excitement, gratitude and joy at such a revelation? This really is Good News. It is truly Gospel.

The heart and the hermitage

To enter this mystery and plumb its depths usually involves some kind of engagement with a desert-hermitage experience. The process of our becoming the persons we are called to be is intensified in the desert experiences in our lives. This is how it was for Jesus. Scripture tells us that when Jesus left the Jordan after his baptism, he was filled with the Holy Spirit and was led by the Spirit into the desert, for forty days being put to the test by the devil. The test engaged Jesus in acknowledging and accepting the poverty of being a human person. What happened during those days of testing in the desert, Johannes Metz describes as three assaults on the poverty Jesus had chosen to embrace as the Word made flesh.[6] The story is probably very familiar to us. Let us meditate on this experience of poverty, its mystery, message and relevance for our lives.

> Then Jesus was led by the Spirit out into the desert to be put to the test by the devil. He fasted for forty days and forty nights, after which he was hungry and the tester came and said to him, 'If you are the Son of God, tell these stones to turn into loaves,' but he replied, 'Scripture says: Human beings live not on bread alone but on every word that comes from the mouth of God.'
>
> The devil then took him to the holy city and set him on the parapet of the Temple. 'If you are the Son of God,' he said,

'throw yourself down; for Scripture says: He has given his angels orders about you, and they will carry you in their arms in case you trip over a stone.'

Jesus said to him, 'Scripture also says: Do not put the Lord your God to the test.'

Next, taking him to a very high mountain, the devil showed him all the kingdoms of the world and their splendour. And he said to him, 'I will give you all these, if you will fall at my feet and do me homage.' Then Jesus replied, 'Away with you, Satan! For Scripture says: The Lord your God is the one to whom you must do homage, him alone you must serve.' Then the devil left him, and suddenly angels appeared and looked after him.

(Mt. 4:1–11)

It was in the desert experience that Jesus entered the mysterious depths of the human heart and faced the innate poverty of the human condition. Metz would go so far as to say that the desert is 'the prototype of man's abject poverty'.[7] This innate poverty is exposed in the three temptations with which Jesus struggled and overcame. The first temptation to turn stones into bread reveals our human tendency to self-sufficiency and security by satisfying our human bodily needs. If our prayer for such immediate satisfaction is not answered then we are tempted to lose trust in the Divine Providence of God. The Israelites of old faced the same temptation in the desert and God responded to their grumbling by supplying manna from heaven. God alone is our ultimate security and Bread of Life.

In our moments of weak faith and proud self-sufficiency, the desert teaches us that Satan lures us into false notions of spiritual strength and unreal expectations of miraculous intervention within our ordinary human limitations. This is subtle and undermines our very nature as human beings. We are not God nor are we equal to God. Jesus laid aside his equality with God and did not give in to the temptation to change the limitations of his humanity; rather he embraced his humanity and showed us how to embrace ours. This is not to say that the miraculous never happens in a human life. We have only to read the Gospels and witness the signs and wonders God worked in and through the ministry of Jesus. But, in this desert experience, Jesus chose to experience the limitations that we all experience as human beings.

We too will have our moments when the poverty of our being impinges painfully upon us in the people and circumstances of our lives. In his temptation to turn stones into bread to fulfil his physical needs, Jesus struggled in his heart to accept the limitations of his humanity. What about our hunger for the fulfilment of our physical needs and the security that comes from this fulfilment? What if God does not seem to alleviate the pain of our human condition? Do we still have faith in the divine *hesed* and do we respond with trust, abandonment and joyful submission to the will of God, even when, or especially when, the ordinary signs of love seem to be lacking in our lives? Can we still believe in love, in the divine *hesed*? The need for 'bread' has many levels of meaning and interpretation. Each of us is invited to experience our poverty and embrace it because this poverty is intrinsic to our creation as human beings.

The second temptation of Jesus came in the form of fulfilling his human need for esteem and popularity. To achieve this, the devil tempted him to jump off the pinnacle of the temple and trust God to save him. The miraculous rescue would win him admiration, popularity and esteem but it would be at the cost of relinquishing his humanity with its limitations and struggles. Calling on his divinity to manipulate the human situation to serve self-centred goals was not the way of Jesus, the Suffering Servant, who chose to become as all men are. Letting go of exaggerated demands for esteem and pleasure from other created beings is part of the struggle in the desert experience. What about our need for recognition, esteem and self-glory? There is aloneness in the embrace of our personal uniqueness and Jesus wrestled with this in his temptation experience.

In the third temptation we see the human need for power and control — sometimes at any cost. The devil invited Jesus to take control of all the kingdoms of the world. Jesus knows that this desire permeates our life in our attempts to control people, events, circumstances and even our own life. We are speaking here of inordinate desire that is manipulative, the very opposite of living in the world of gift. The only appropriate response to the gift of God's life and love is praise and thanksgiving. In other words: worship. 'The Lord your God is the one to whom you must do homage, him alone you must serve' (Mt. 4:11).

This third temptation tested the relationship between Jesus and his Father, a relationship that was at the heart of his identity. 'In worshipping God man is brought totally before himself and to himself. Thus prayer is the ultimate realization of man. Surrendering everything, even his poverty, he becomes truly rich: For when I am weak, then I am strong.'[8] In the temptations in the desert, Jesus remained steadfast and loyal, those characteristics so evident in a living and loving *hesed* relationship. This relationship is tenderly revealed and exposed towards the end of Jesus' earthly life when love, trust, abandonment and joyful surrender were the hallmarks of his final days and hours.

The poverty, humility and patient suffering in the circumstances surrounding the birth of Jesus and lived out in the hidden years in Nazareth, tried and tested in the temptations, reaches a climax in his death on the Cross.

> But he emptied himself,
> taking the form of a slave,
> becoming as human beings are,
> and being in every way like a human being
> he was humbler yet,
> even to accepting death, death on a cross. (Phil. 2: 6–8)

Self-emptying through poverty, humbler yet, even to the patient suffering on the Cross – this is the ultimate in self-giving, sacrificial love, abandonment, joyful submission to the Will of God and active charity towards others. This is the revelation of the *hesed* of God and the perfect response in and through the God-man, Jesus Christ.

On the Cross, the faith and mercy so closely associated with the divine *hesed* are fully lived and expressed in the human life of Jesus. Faith: his total commitment in unconditional love and total trust, abandoning life itself into the hands and heart of God. Mercy: the tender, compassionate, forgiving and sacrificial love in the heart of God, poured out on all creation in and through the crucified love on the Cross. This is the God revealed in Jesus the

Word made flesh. This is the God of covenant-love who chose to be poor, humble and crucified for love's sake. This is the God who captivated the heart of St Francis.

The heart of Francis

A baby with tiny finger-nails, a man bleeding and thirsty nailed to rough wood, a small white wafer held high for veneration. Little, powerless, silent. Manger, cross, bread. Bethlehem, Calvary, Eucharist. To Francis of Assisi these said everything about God's love for us and they formed the axis of his holiness.[9]

These words of the late Eric Doyle, OFM, form our starting point for discovering the heart of Francis and his relationship with God in Jesus. Gazing in wonder at the Word made flesh in Jesus Christ so captivated the heart of Francis that he re-enacted the Bethlehem scene in the mountain cave of Greccio. His first biographer, Brother Thomas of Celano,[10] gives a graphic description of the way in which Francis re-enacted and celebrated the stupendous mystery of the Incarnation. Using real people from the village of Greccio and real animals, on that Christmas Eve at Midnight Mass, Francis brought Bethlehem alive in the cave of Greccio.

There simplicity is given a place of honour,
poverty is exalted,
humility is commended,
and out of Greccio is made a new Bethlehem.[11]

The poverty and humility in the heart of the baby of Bethlehem was already eternally present in the heart of the eternal Father. This is the *hesed* of God made manifest in littleness, poverty and humility and only the Son who is nearest the Father's heart could reveal this to us. One of the many words used by Scripture scholars to interpret *hesed* is tenderness. How fitting an interpretation when we speak of the Babe of Bethlehem.

The tender, humble love of the Father would reach its climax in the poverty and dereliction of the Cross. There on the Cross, the heart of Jesus was pierced, opened wide to reveal the heart of the Father and his steadfast, merciful love for each one of us in Christ. Such a manifestation of humble love would be inconceivable without the human manifestation of this love in Jesus Christ. This is the mystery of the heart of God and the mystery of the human heart. This is the mystery that formed the heart of Francis and had far-reaching consequences for his life.

In answering the call to return love for love, Thomas of Celano tells us: 'So thoroughly did the humility of the Incarnation and the charity of the Passion occupy his memory that he scarcely wanted to think of anything else.'[12] This interiorizing of the Word of God fulfilled in Francis his personal vocation to become the person God had intended from all eternity. The personal vocation of each person is unique and unrepeatable. Each of us grows into our identity by gazing on the Word made flesh in Jesus. Like St Francis, we need to have him before our eyes, on our lips and in our hearts. This is what Thomas of Celano said of Francis:

> The brothers who lived with him know
> that daily, constantly, talk of Jesus was always on his lips,
> *sweet and pleasant* conversations about him,
> kind words full of love.
> *Out of the fullness of the heart his mouth spoke.*
> So the spring of radiant love
> that filled his heart within
> gushed forth.
> He was always with Jesus:
> Jesus in his heart,
> Jesus in his mouth,
> Jesus in his ears,
> Jesus in his eyes,
> Jesus in his hands,
> He bore Jesus always in his whole body.[13]

This love of Jesus reached its climax in the life of St Francis when, spending forty days on La Verna, Francis prayed:

O my Lord Jesus Christ, two graces do I pray thee to grant unto me before I die: the first, that while I live I may feel in my body and in my soul, so far as is possible, that sorrow, sweet Lord, that thou didst suffer in the hour of thy most bitter passion; the second, that I may feel in my heart, as far as may be possible, that exceeding love wherewith, O Son of God, thou wast enkindled to endure willingly for us sinners agony so great.[14]

The Lord answered the prayer of Francis in an extraordinary way. He was totally transformed into Christ Crucified, bearing in his frail body the very wounds of his crucified Saviour. The heart of Francis and the heart of Christ were one. Solitude had produced in Francis that total conversion of heart whereby his whole person was one with Christ. Francis embraced the human condition including the suffering that marks every human life in one way or another. Reflecting on the La Verna experience, Sr Frances Teresa remarks: 'Indeed, the image of Christ as love in pain, spells out for us that our suffering is greatly honoured by God, that our pain is received with reverence and taken right into the being of the Godhead and somehow made a part of that divine life.'[15] How comforting and consoling for us when we struggle with the pain and suffering within our own lives and in the lives of others.

Almost immediately after his momentous and mystical experience of union with the love and suffering of the God-man, Jesus Christ, St Francis, moved with compassion, burned with zeal to preach and show mercy. Is not this the human *hesed* response, love reaching out to our brothers and sisters as compassion and mercy? The long journey that Francis made into his own heart, into the hearts of others and into the heart of God is your journey too. It will engage you in a compassionate love that purifies, heals, transforms, unites and leads to adoration. Are you ready?

Our hearts

The journey into the mystery of the heart of God and our own hearts is a choice and a challenge that we cannot afford to neglect. Within every heart, whether a person is aware of it or not, there is a spiritual quest for the fullness of life and love. The often-repeated words of St Augustine are well known and probably familiar to you: Our hearts are restless, until they rest in Thee.

What is the state of your heart right now as you read this? I suggest that you stay with this question long enough to identify the condition of your own heart.

Jesus was emphatic about the importance of our heart's condition. He referred to it as soil or earth into which his Word gently falls. Perhaps you remember the parable of the Seed of the Word of God. In this parable Jesus is at pains to help us to understand the relationship that exists between his Word and our hearts. He said:

> A sower went out to sow his seed.
> Now as he sowed, some fell on the edge of the path and was trampled on; and the birds ate it up.
> Some seed fell on rock, and when it sprang up it withered away, having no moisture. Some seed fell in the middle of thorns and the thorns grew up with it and choked it.
> And some seed fell into good soil and grew and produced its crop a hundredfold. (Lk. 8:4–8)

The disciples asked Jesus to explain this parable. He said:

> The seed is the word of God.
> Those on the edge of the path are people who have heard it, and then the devil comes and carries away the word from their hearts in case they should believe and be saved.
> Those on the rock are people who, when they first hear it, welcome the word with joy. But these have no root; they believe for a while, and in time of trial they give up.
> As for the part that fell in thorns, this is people who have heard, but as they go on their way they are choked by the worries and riches and pleasures of life and never produce any crops.
> As for the part in the rich soil, this is people with a noble and generous heart who have heard the word and take it to themselves and yield a harvest through their perseverance.   (Lk. 8:11–15)

In the parable Jesus draws attention to specific characteristics that prevent the growth and fulfilment of the relationship between his Word and our hearts. This relationship can only become reality in and through Christ, the image of the invisible God and the First-born of all creation (Col. 1:15–17). He is the perfect revelation of the heart of God and the perfect revelation of the heart of a child of God. As the eternal masterpiece of God's creation, Christ is the First Adorer and Perfect Child.[16]

To become an adorer presupposes a pure heart and to become a perfect child presupposes a humble heart that recognizes its innate poverty and dependence on the Father and source of all being. Jesus said: 'Blessed are the poor in spirit: theirs is the kingdom of Heaven' and 'Blessed are the pure in heart: they shall see God' (Mt. 5:3, 8). Our hearts, created to receive the Word of God, are totally dependent upon grace to become his dwelling place. Jesus uses the familiar and tender word 'home' to describe what happens when we take his Word to heart in love.

> Anyone who loves me will keep my word,
> and my Father will love him,
> and we shall come to him
> and make a home in him. (Jn.14:23)

'Come to me, all you who labour and are overburdened, and I will give you rest ... Learn from me, for I am gentle and humble in heart' (Mt. 11:28–9). What a wonderful invitation from Jesus! No matter what you have discovered within your heart, the invitation is for you, now. 'Come to me,' Jesus says. This is a first step. Jesus does not force anyone to respond. An invitation is a call from one person to another, leaving the one invited free to respond or not. If you freely draw near to the heart of Jesus, then you may wish to listen attentively to the following words which are a personal message for you. Deeply embedded in the invitation to 'Come and learn' heart-to-heart is the lure of the desert, the privileged place of trysting and testing which is our focus for Chapter 3.

Invitations to Prayer

Words of Love
1. Come to me, all you who labour and are overburdened, and I will give you rest. (Mt. 11:28)
2. If you only knew what God is offering ... (Jn. 4:10)

3. In all truth I tell you, whoever listens to my words, and believes in the one who sent me, has eternal life. (Jn. 5:24)

4. The words I have spoken to you are spirit and they are life. (Jn. 6:63)

5. Let anyone who is thirsty come to me!
   Let anyone who believes in me come and drink! (Jn. 7:37)

6. If you make my word your home you will indeed be my disciples; you will come to know the truth, and the truth will set you free. (Jn. 8:31–2)

7. Do not let your hearts be troubled. You trust in God, trust also in me. (Jn. 14:1)

8. I am the Way; I am Truth and Life. (Jn. 14:6)

9. Anyone who has seen me has seen the Father. (Jn. 14:9)

10. I shall not leave you orphans; I shall come to you. (Jn. 14:18)

11. I have loved you just as the Father has loved me. (Jn. 15:9)

12. Look, I am with you always; yes, to the end of time. (Mt. 28:20)

Heart Reflections

1. Pray with St John's Gospel 1:18. Meditate on Jesus nearest the Father's heart. Seek to enter into the mystery of Jesus revealing to you the mystery of your own heart and the mystery of the heart of God.

2. Read Mark 8:27–33. Now place yourself in the presence of Jesus and hear him address these words to you: '*N*, . . . who am I for you?' When you have answered Jesus' question to you, continue the conversation by asking Jesus the question: 'Jesus, who am I for you?'

3. Jesus said: 'Wherever your treasure is, there will your heart be too' (Mt. 6:21). What do you treasure most in this life? Health? Wealth? Beauty? Status? Esteem? Affection? Power? Family? Friends? Love? Faith? God? Stay with the truth of the connection between treasure and your heart. Your response?

4. Jesus described himself as 'gentle and humble in heart' (Mt. 11:29). Explore the quality of gentleness – its meaning and expression in your own life in relationship to yourself, to others, to creation and to God. Then explore the quality of humility in the same way. Can you identify what hinders and

what helps the growth and development of gentleness and
humility in your heart?

Praying with the Psalms

Psalm 49

Hear this, all peoples!
Give ear, all inhabitants of the
earth,
both low and high,
rich and poor together!
My mouth shall speak wisdom!
the meditation of my heart
shall be understanding.
I will incline my ear to the Word;
I will solve my problems
through the whispers
of the Heart's voice.

Why should I give up in times of
trouble,
when the stubbornness of my fears
surround me,
Fears that give birth to greed
and lead to exploitation?

Truly I cannot save myself,
or offer a haven of peace to
another,
When my home is like a hornet's nest,
a hive of restless fears.
Turning to you, O Guiding Spirit,
is my strength and support,
a stronghold in times of trouble.

Yes, even the wise are not immune
to fear;
yet, unlike the ignorant, the wise
face their fears with resolve.
Not running away, nor projecting them
onto others,

They trace them to the source,
rooting them out as weeds
from a rose garden.
Thus, they do not trust in the riches
of the world,
but in the Treasure hidden
in the heart.

Others are arrogant in their ignorance,
proud of their own counsel.
Like sheep led to slaughter,
their fears compel them to
walk in darkness,
Guiding them onto unholy paths,
into webs of intrigue,
where despair and destruction
make their home.
Yet does the Spirit of Truth abide within,
veiled by bulwarks of pain.
Be not afraid to discover the Treasure
within,
to seek the gold hidden in
the garden of your heart.
For inasmuch as you root out
each fear,
will truth and peace and joy
become your riches.
You will live in the realm of Love
becoming a light,
a beneficial presence in the world.
Future generations will be blessed,
the bonds of ignorance
broken forever.
O Spirit of Truth, You are our strength
and our guiding light,
Leading us to the eternal Treasure,
the Heart of our heart.

Psalm 134

Come, bask in the Light of Love,
all you who would serve
the Divine Plan!
Lift up your hands to the Holy One,
singing songs of praise!
Bow down and receive blessing from
the Giver of Life!
All praises be to You,
whose Love created heaven
and earth![17]

Praying with St Francis

Prayer and Thanksgiving

All-powerful, most holy,
Almighty and supreme God,
Holy and just *Father*,
Lord King of *heaven and earth*
we thank You for Yourself
for through Your holy will
and through Your only Son
with the Holy Spirit
You have created everything spiritual and corporal
and, after making us in *Your own image and likeness*,
You placed us in paradise.

Through our own fault we fell.

We thank You
for as through Your Son You created us,
so through Your holy love
with which You loved us
You brought about His birth
as true God and true man
by the glorious, ever-virgin, most blessed, holy Mary
and You willed to redeem us captives
through His cross and blood and death. . . .

We humbly ask
our Lord Jesus Christ,
Your *beloved Son,*

in Whom You were well pleased,
together with the Holy Spirit,
the Paraclete,
to give You thanks, for everything
as it pleases You and Him,
Who always satisfies You in everything,
through Whom You have done so much for us.
Alleluia![18]

Notes

1. 'The Prayer before the Crucifix', in Armstrong *et al.*, *Francis of Assisi*, vol.1, p. 40.
2. Metz, *Poverty of Spirit*, p. 9.
3. When we speak of *hesed* in relation to God, it expresses his unconditional, gratuitous, benevolent, grace-filled, merciful, tender, self-giving, self-emptying, steadfast and enduring love for every person. This divine *hesed* calls for corresponding *hesed* among human beings, consisting of self-giving, loving trust, abandonment, deep affection, piety, a love in short which is a joyful submission to the will of God and an active charity towards others.
4. Metz, *Poverty of Spirit*, p. 24.
5. Delio, *Simply Bonaventure*, p. 85.
6. Metz, *Poverty of Spirit*, p. 14.
7. Ibid., p. 16.
8. Ibid., p. 53.
9 Raischl and Cirino, *My Heart's Quest*, p. 158.
10. 'The Life of Saint Francis by Thomas of Celano', in Armstrong *et al.*, *Francis of Assisi*, vol. 1, pp. 254–7.
11. Ibid., p. 255.
12. Ibid., p. 254.
13. 'The Life of Saint Francis by Thomas of Celano', in Armstrong *et al.*, *Francis of Assisi*, vol. 1, p. 283.
14. 'Third Consideration on the Sacred Stigmata', in Habig, *Omnibus of Sources*, p. 1444.
15. Frances Teresa, OSC, *Living the Incarnation*, p. 101.
16. Foley *et al.*, *To Live as Francis Lived*, p. 23.
17. Merrill, *Psalms For Praying*, pp. 94–6, 282.
18. 'The Earlier Rule', in Armstrong *et al.*, *Francis of Assisi*, vol. 1, p. 81.

Chapter 3

Beauty and Brokenness

WE INTRODUCED THE DESERT as the place of love, intimacy, betrothal and marriage. This symbolic and spousal language helped us to enter into the passionate, tender, merciful, steadfast love with which we are always loved. It is always so. It is the divine *hesed*. Nothing and no one can change this wonderful truth about our existence. In the silence and solitude of the desert-hermitage of your own heart you have treasured words of love spoken from the heart of our loving and compassionate God. Within the security of such love, perhaps you are now ready to enter more deeply into your own heart to engage with the desert-hermitage experience in the process of purification and growth.

To plumb the depths of the heart will lead you, sooner or later, into a place where the secret of solitude will be revealed. Some people call this a desert or hermitage experience. In this sacred place, we touch not only our own hearts but also the heart of God, which will in turn lead us to the hearts of our brothers and sisters and to the whole of creation. An adventure awaits you if you have the heart for it! But be prepared for a challenge.

The image of the desert is a familiar one in sacred and secular literature. It is the place of challenge and change when we are brought face to face with the mystery of our own hearts. The poet, Gerard Manley Hopkins, in his personal desert of desolation and doubt, emptiness and pain, cried out:

My own heart let me more have pity on; let
Me live my sad self hereafter kind,
Charitable; not live this tormented mind
With this tormented mind tormenting yet.

I cast for comfort I can no more get
By groping round my comfortless, than blind
Eyes in their dark can day or thirst can find
Thirsts all in all in a world of wet.[1]

This is the other face of the desert experience, one that is not comfortable and cosy, intimate and spousal. The desert is the place where the heart is not only lured and loved, it is also tried and tested. This is the twofold process in which we are invited to embrace both the trysting and the testing. Shakespeare hints at this two-sided process in the play *As You Like It* where he says: 'Sweet are the uses of adversity ... there is much matter to be heard and learn'd.' This desert process is harrowing in its purification and frightening in its relentless hold to bring us to greater heart awareness. Such awareness will eventually lead us to enjoy in ever-greater depth the wonder of our being, forever embraced in the heart of God. Perhaps this is why the lure of the desert has always been part of the human struggle towards healing and wholeness.

There is a mystery of personal identity and unconditional love here, the acceptance of which, in Christian terms, leads to the thrilling awareness of seeing ourselves with the eyes of faith, as unique reflections of God and infinitely and always loved by him. To arrive at this awareness and acceptance requires a lot of inner work: 'heart work'. It is a costly undertaking. The poet, Yeats once said that the starting point for such an undertaking is 'the rag and bone shop of the heart'. But the joy of discovery far outweighs the struggle involved and another poet, Herbert, reminds us:

God doth supply the want,
As when the heart says (sighing to be approved)
Oh, could I love! and stops:
God writeth, Loved.[2]

The heart of God

Loved! This word, this experience says it all. Discovering such excessive and extravagant love in the person of Jesus takes us deeply into the realm of mystery and grace. Reflecting on the human life of Jesus leads us to a realization of just how costly such love is, and the desert experience sets the scene in graphic terms.

The response of Jesus in his desert experience paved the way for his continuing engagement in the human journey. This whole-hearted engagement reveals our dignity as human beings created in the image and likeness of God, and it also reveals the heart of the God whose image and likeness we are called to express. Jesus, the one who is nearest the Father's heart, reveals to us the divine reality in which we are enfolded. Jesus came among us and revealed to us a God who is a Trinity of Father, Son and Holy Spirit whose heart is revealed in the divine *hesed* relationship of saviour, shepherd, servant, brother, bridegroom, beloved, healer, father, mother and friend, climaxed in crucified Love on the Cross. Here we are immersed in a sea of significant relationships that are part of the mystery of who we are and who God is.

The scriptural images of God we have already mentioned, explicitly convey the tenderness of the divine *hesed* relationship in a human life of self-giving, self-emptying, self-surrendering, sacrificial love. 'No one can have greater love than to lay down his life for his friends' (Jn. 15:13). The heart of God revealed in Jesus, holds nothing back. Love gives all. Perhaps you may wish to take one or more of the images mentioned and allow the tenderness of the heart of God to touch your life in and through each revelation. Such tenderness and unconditional love may give you courage to embrace the beauty and brokenness revealed in the depths of your own heart.

The heart and the hermitage

The temptations of Jesus that we pondered in the previous chapter, face each of us with the stark realization of what it means to be human and what is involved in the process of becoming fully human. Such engagement is intensified in the desert-hermitage experience. Jesus did not take any shortcuts in the process of growing to maturity and he calls each of us to follow the same course in our own individual way. 'If anyone wants to be a follower of mine, let him renounce himself and take up his cross and follow me' (Mk. 8: 34). Your cross is a personal cross. My cross is a personal cross. It is the cross of bearing patiently the process of growing into the maturity of a fully human, fully alive human being.

The way to wholeness is not an easy option and the desert-hermitage experience highlights the choices and challenges that are involved. These choices and challenges lie deep within our hearts. According to the prophet Jeremiah: 'The heart is more devious than any other thing' (Jer. 17:9), and Jesus following the same tradition noted: 'For from the heart come evil intentions: murder, adultery, fornication, theft, perjury, slander' (Mt. 15:19) and evil speech: 'For words flow out of what fills the heart' (Mt. 12:34). How necessary it is for us to know the condition of our hearts.

In the early Church the most notable advocate of the desert experience in the formation of the heart is St Antony (AD 251–356). This is what he says: 'For one who wishes to live in the solitude of the desert there is only one conflict and that is with the heart.'[3] This connection between the desert and the conflict within the heart had already been made by Origen (AD 185–254) when he said:

> We shall not fight, as men in former times fought, nor will our battles be against men on earth, but against principalities and authorities, against the cosmic powers of this dark world. So now you know where you have to fight battles like this ... We must bestir ourselves to do battle, but against those enemies which come forth from our own hearts, evil thoughts, thefts, lies about other people, blasphemies, and all other enemies of our own soul that are like them.[4]

This implies that the desert-hermitage experience brings us face to face with the ambiguous and dark areas of our heart that would remain unknown or unheeded in the normal course of our busy lives. A challenge indeed! To explore these areas requires both courage and discipline but most of all the grace (*hesed*) of God and the activity of the Holy Spirit. What is the next step in exploring these unredeemed areas of our hearts? Presuming you desire to enter more deeply on the heart's journey, having set aside a time and place to meet God in prayer and reflection, perhaps the first step is to ask humbly for the grace to see the landscape of your heart, those secret thoughts and motivations known only to God.

It may interest you to know that the word 'heart' is used 176 times in the New Testament with emphasis on the heart as the life-giving centre of the human person. Thus the heart is the inner core of your feelings, intellect and will. As such it remains the place of symbol and mystery and of freedom and grace. Of the forty-eight times Jesus uses the word heart, he emphasizes both the positive and the negative characteristics involved. That there are negative aspects implies the need for conversion, and the first invitation of Jesus after his own confrontation in the desert was: 'Repent, and believe the Gospel' (Mk. 1:15). Neither aspects of this invitation stand alone. Therefore, you may have to ask yourself the question: What do I need to repent of and what is the Good News I am called to believe in?

If you have accompanied Jesus in his desert experience, then you will understand that repentance involves an inner struggle between your false self and your true self. Your true self is your unique creation in the image and likeness of God and you come to fulfilment through your relationship with him. He is the source of your being, the purpose of your life and the goal of your journey. Your false self is constructed and developed without reference to God as your origin, purpose and destiny. The intensity of this painful process is summed up by St Augustine in his *Confessions*: 'And so the two wills fought it out – the old and the new, the one carnal, the other spiritual – and in their struggle tore my soul apart.'[5]

Based and built on illusion, the false self makes itself the centre and endeavours to mask the illusion with symbols of pleasure, power and possessions. These were the three temptations Jesus faced and overcame in his desert experience; you too will struggle with these basic instincts and desires in your own way and within your own circumstances. This innate selfishness is manifested in a heart that is closed to God; a heart whose spiritual eyes are blind and whose spiritual ears are deaf to the overwhelming love, beauty and goodness of the heart of God revealed in Jesus Christ.

Using the richly symbolic language of treasure, Jesus said: 'Wherever your treasure is, there will your heart be too' (Mt. 6:21). Linger with the image of treasure. It is precious. Often it is hidden. It usually involves a hero or heroine struggling with a perilous and adventurous journey of discovery. Are you prepared to venture into hitherto unknown regions where you may be beset by trials and tribulations in order to find the treasure that lies hidden within your own heart? It is in the deep recesses of the heart that we discover both our beauty and our brokenness. Such was the discovery of St Francis when he seriously set out on his heart's journey.

The heart of Francis

The symbol of the heart is the key for unlocking the symbolic universe of Francis. Within ten of his writings, Francis refers to the heart forty-eight times and, following the example of Jesus, he recognizes both positive and negative characteristics associated with the heart and its condition. We have already pointed out that Francis uses the word 'heart' more than all others to describe the reality and the quality of our relationship with God and the consequences for all other relationships.

At the very beginning of his conversion, Francis prayed before the Crucifix of San Damiano for enlightenment in his darkness of heart. The status symbols in which Francis was immersed left a lasting influence on him but his pursuit of wealth, status, power and prestige left him searching, dissatisfied and unfulfilled. We know that Francis experienced a period of solitude and silence after the collapse of his worldly ambitions. It was a time of deep personal reflection. This pattern of collapse, reflection and new insights was familiar to Francis and probably it is familiar to every person on the journey of life. No one is exempt from the disappointments, disasters, failures and foibles that test the quality of our hearts. Reflection in itself does not bring about new insights and desired change. Solitude, chosen or imposed – the latter in Francis' case through illness and being a prisoner of war – may be the occasion for enlightenment. As one of Francis' biographers, St Bonaventure writes:

> And because *affliction can enlighten* spiritual *awareness, the hand of the Lord was upon him*, and *a change of the right hand of the Most High*, afflicting his body with prolonged illness in order to prepare his soul for the anointing of the Holy Spirit.[6]

Face to face with his own limitations, Francis at first experienced these limits physically. We know that as a young and ambitious man, Francis greatly cherished bodily health, sumptuous garments, fancy foods, the pleasures of friendship, fame, popularity, glory and honour and the world of nature. In solitude, Francis had to reassess all that he held dear. As his biographer, Thomas of Celano tells us: 'It is difficult to leave familiar things behind, and things once instilled in the spirit are not easily weakened.'[7]

Therefore, he sought out a quiet place away from the tumult of his usual affairs and prayed with all his heart that God would reveal his purpose. The upheavals in his life gave Francis the opportunity to stand back from his usual way of behaving and thinking but it was not easy for him. Listen again to Thomas of Celano as he describes Francis' struggle in caves and dungeons, secluded spots and solitary places, all the while his heart a battleground.

> He prayed with all his heart that the eternal and true God guide his way and *teach him to do his will*. He endured great suffering in his soul, and he was not able to rest until he accomplished in action what he had conceived in his heart. Different thoughts followed one another, and their relentlessness severely disturbed him.[8]

Perhaps each of us can identify with this experience of Francis. The process of purification and the clarity that emerges does not come all at once. What is clear is that the heart, its conversion to love and the place of solitude in that process act upon one

another. In other words, heart, *hesed* (both divine and human) and
hermitage are intimately linked. Here the depth and dynamics of
the inner journey challenge us to face our innate selfishness and
motivation, inviting us to accept God for who he is and not who
we imagine him to be within the limitations of our own thoughts
and desires.

Aware of the fragility and weakness of our humanity, Francis
advises us to pray and not lose heart on this spiritual adventure.
He very explicitly warns us of the deceptions we encounter along
the way. In his parable on the heart, which we find in *The Earlier
Rule*, Francis spells out very clearly the ways of the evil one and
draws our attention to the need for care and vigilance.

> And let us beware of the malice and craftiness of Satan, who does
> not want anyone to turn his mind and heart to God. And prowl-
> ing around he wants to ensnare a person's heart under the guise
> of some reward or assistance, to choke out the word and precepts
> of the Lord from our memory, and desiring a person's heart, he
> wants to blind it through worldly affairs and concerns and to live
> there ...[9]

Through many years of on-going exposure to the love of God
revealed in Jesus, through the circumstances of his life with the
brothers, with Clare and her sisters, and with the lay penitents,
Francis seems to have grasped the nature and pattern of our resistance and attraction to the Gospel way. Although Francis does not
lead the life of a solitary hermit, solitude and time spent in the
hermitage became increasingly important to him. That he wrote
a *Rule for Hermitages* emphasizes the importance of the eremitical
life in the life of Francis and his followers. In that document
Francis inserted only one biblical text. Significantly it was the text
relating to seeking the Kingdom and its justice. 'And let them
seek *first* of all the Kingdom of God and his justice' (Mt. 6: 33).

St Bonaventure, friar and biographer of St Francis, takes the
theme of justice and explains it as the restoration of beauty.
'Justice makes beautiful what had been deformed, it makes more
beautiful what was already beautiful, and most beautiful what had
been improved.'[10] The absence of justice is the absence of beauty.
In biblical language 'doing justice' is essential to the living of the

covenant relationship that is characterized by *hesed*, that steadfast, merciful love named compassion. Such compassionate living restores right relationships with oneself, others, creation and God. This is the insight of Francis in proclaiming the centrality of justice in his *Rule for Hermitages*.

Matthew Fox points out that people 'tend to ignore the mystery and riches of solitude where so much compassion is learned and developed'.[11] The experience of Francis in the solitude of caves and hermitages confirms this insight. Fox would go so far as to say that 'compassion is the biblical word for contemplation'.[12] If 'doing justice' is the restoration of beauty through compassionate living then the example of Francis in his active-contemplative rhythm points us in the direction of wholeness, harmony and integration.

The value of the desert-hermitage experience in purifying the heart and exposing one to the divine *hesed* is emphasized particularly in the experience of St Francis on Mount La Verna. His heart would pass through the crucible of suffering leading him to a total identification with his crucified and compassionate Lord. This happened towards the end of his life in response to his prayer for total union with Jesus. Francis prayed:

> O my Lord Jesus Christ, two graces do I pray thee to grant unto me before I die: the first, that while I live I may feel in my body and in my soul, so far as is possible, that sorrow, sweet Lord, that thou didst suffer in the hour of thy most bitter passion; the second that I may feel in my heart, as far as may be possible, that exceeding love wherewith, O Son of God, thou wast enkindled to endure willingly for us sinners agony so great.[13]

The Lord answered the prayer of Francis in an extraordinary way. He was totally transformed into Christ Crucified, bearing in his body the very wounds of his crucified Saviour. The heart of Francis and the heart of Christ were one. Solitude had produced in Francis that total conversion and transformation of heart whereby his whole person was one with Christ. Almost immediately after this momentous and mystical encounter, Francis, moved with compassion, burned with zeal to preach and to show mercy (*hesed*). After receiving the stigmata, Francis 'burned with a great desire to return to the humility he practiced at the beginning; to nurse the lepers as he did at the outset'.[14] It was his experience of his compassionate Lord that transformed the heart of Francis and made his body into a living crucifix.

> For when he was taken above in the seraphic ardor of desires into God and into Him, he who, by a boundless love, wanted to be crucified, was transformed by a compassionate sweetness.[15]

Francis had a keen awareness of the heart and its ways and it is part of his genius to move us into an awareness of the dynamics from within, from the heart, which shape our lives. From within that awareness, Francis now invites you to radical conversion of heart and transformation.

Our hearts

A good starting place for the journey of discovery into your heart is the Beatitudes. One interpretation of Beatitude is happiness. Where do you seek happiness? In this answer lies a clue to the choices and challenges you may be required to face as you journey towards healing and wholeness. The Beatitudes do not deny our human instincts, emotions, thinking and willing but they do invite us to reorder or restructure them according to their God-given capacities. In biblical language this is the painful journey of *metanoia*, or conversion. The human journey of the heart is the movement from selfish love to selfless and unconditional love but the initiative comes from God. God is always the first to reach out and approach the human person and he is the last to go away.[16]

In reaching out to us and becoming one of us, Jesus entered into the human condition, which the Fathers of the Church often referred to as the region of unlikeness. In and through Christ and his desert experience, which would culminate in his desert experience on Calvary, the Holy Spirit sought to restore in the human heart the image and likeness of God, lost by sin and the refusal to love. Beauty and brokenness! How vital for each of us to enter this realm of mystery and grace.

The journey of our hearts through the different types of desert experiences in our lives restores the image and likeness provided we engage in what is involved. Are you ready to face the unmasking and dismantling of false notions of love and life that may be lurking in your heart? If you are, then take time to meditate on the Beatitudes.

> How blessed are the poor in spirit:
> the kingdom of Heaven is theirs.
> Blessed are the gentle:
> they shall have the earth as inheritance.
> Blessed are those who mourn:
> they shall be comforted.
> Blessed are those who hunger and thirst for uprightness:
> they shall have their fill.
> Blessed are the merciful:
> they shall have mercy shown them.
> Blessed are the pure in heart:
> they shall see God.
> Blessed are the peacemakers:
> they shall be recognised as children of God.
> Blessed are those who are persecuted in the cause of uprightness:
> the kingdom of Heaven is theirs. (Mt. 5:3–10)

This is a perfect description of the journey of restoration of the image and likeness in which we were created. The beauty portrayed in the Beatitudes is a yardstick for you to measure the areas of brokenness that are still operative within your heart. Perhaps you may wish to reflect on each one separately in order to see how the Beatitudes address your false symbols of security, power and self-esteem that the false self struggles to satisfy.

Our starting point is the heart. Blessed are the pure in heart: they shall see God. What an astonishing promise! The purity Jesus speaks of in this Beatitude presupposes a heart where affections, intellect and will are integrated in a love that is a participation in the life of God himself. Susan Muto states that this Beatitude touches upon 'foundational longings in the human spirit: one is singleness and the other seeing'.[17] She suggests that the first addresses the human desire to move from fragmentation to integration and the second addresses the desire to let go of illusion and live in reality. No one reaches this stage of Beatitude without the suffering which purification entails, the process we call conversion and which is intimately linked to the desert-hermitage experience. Adrian Van Kaam speaks of this when he says: 'The release of the Christ form in our whole being and world is only possible to the degree that our hearts have been formed and reformed in his likeness and transformed by his grace.'[18] We cannot avoid those two human experiences, which touch every life: love and suffering, and this is the ground plan that is revealed in the Beatitudes.

Let us look closely at the process of becoming pure in heart that the promise of seeing God may become a reality in our lives. The desert-hermitage experience highlights the many stages and confrontations that are essential in the movement towards healing and integration but nothing happens unless and until God takes the initiative. In the Christian tradition it is always God who moves first in reaching out to humanity. This initiative is rooted in the *hesed* of God in the covenant-love relationship.

The process of entering the mystery of our hearts and persevering in the battle against all forms of self-seeking love requires a radical conversion that enables us to see differently: from God's point of view. Scripture uses the term 'eyes and ears of the heart' to underscore attentive listening and effective hearing. The development of the spiritual senses, especially our ability to see and hear, to look and to listen, is a rich biblical theme and Jesus quoted the prophet Isaiah in this respect. 'They may look and look, but never perceive; listen and listen, but never understand; to avoid changing their ways and being healed' (Mk. 4:12). The goal of purification is to behold the face of God and this is God's desire for us. 'He wants to show his face to those who have purified, not their eyes of flesh but the eyes of their hearts.'[19]

Likewise, regarding the ears of the heart, Augustine knew how easy it is to close the ears of the heart to the voice of God and open them to 'the wiles of the enemy'.[20] He stressed the necessity of being attentive to the Bridegroom's voice. 'Be not vain, my soul, and take care that the ear of your heart be not deafened by the din of your vanity. You must listen ...'[21] Augustine made this prayerful plea: 'Say to my soul, I am your salvation. Say it so that I can hear it. My heart is listening, Lord; open the ears of my heart and say to my soul, I am your salvation.'[22]

Just as the physical senses are strengthened by regular practice, so too with the spiritual senses, and this is where the desert is significant. It is a journey inward where our natural God-given powers are transformed in the holy warfare that ensues when conversion is taken seriously. 'The battle you are to fight is within you; within you is that wicked city that must be overthrown; your enemy comes out of your own heart. It is not I who say it, but Christ.'[23] To engage in this spiritual battle involves digging, pruning and cultivating the soil of the heart. St Ephrem reminds us that Christ is the One who tills the soil of the heart; our part is to co-operate by being attentive, responsive and receptive. 'Blessed be the Husbandman, by Whom the ground of the heart is tilled.'[24]

Jesus spoke of the soil of the heart where both wheat and weeds abound. We have only to think of the parable of the darnel. Good seed was sown but while everyone was asleep the enemy came, and sowed darnel among the wheat, and made off. There are several lessons to be learned from this parable in Matthew 13:24–30. First, there was only good seed sown. This is a comforting truth. We are all created good. We are created in the image and likeness of God who is all Goodness and Love. Is this how you see your creation? If not, why not? What has happened to cloud the reality of your personal and innate goodness?

The parable says that when everyone was asleep, the enemy came. The lesson here is to be vigilant. 'More than all else, keep watch over your heart, since here are the wellsprings of life' (Pr. 4:23). It is important to be vigilant because what is sown will come up and as Jesus said: 'Make a tree sound and its fruit will be sound; make a tree rotten and its fruit will be rotten. For the tree can be told by its fruit' (Mt. 12: 33–4). It is interesting that this parable is related in the context of the words that come forth from our hearts. Jesus was speaking to the Pharisees when he said: 'You brood of vipers, how can your speech be good when you are evil? For words flow out from what fills the heart' (Mt. 12:34). St Augustine says this in another way: 'You can have a word in your heart, as it were a design born in your mind, so that your mind brings forth the design; and the design is, so to speak, the offspring of your mind, the child of your heart.'[25] Keeping watch over our hearts will involve vigilance regarding thoughts that give rise to words, which in turn become deeds.

In the whole area of discerning of spirits we cannot be too simplistic. One modern author, Richard Rohr, points out that the process of discerning the weeds is not an easy task because 'the only way the enemy succeeds is by disguising himself'. Rohr is convinced that the parable of the darnel is one of the most important and neglected parables in the Christian tradition. Rohr would advise us to 'go gently on the weeds' because subtlety and paradox are not easy for us to grasp and it is easy to mistake the wheat for the weeds and vice versa.[26] How important it is for us to be in touch with the inner motivations of our hearts. Truly the Beatitudes reveal to us both the dark and unredeemed areas of our hearts together with the challenges we face in allowing God to make us new in heart and spirit.

How blessed are the poor in spirit. In the temptations Jesus resisted the immediate fulfilment of basic human needs to teach us about our innate and radical poverty before God. Do you find radical poverty and dependence on God easy or difficult? In what way do you actually experience yourself as a poor person? How do you try to avoid or falsify the poverty you experience as a person? I am not talking here of poverty and deprivation that prevents a person from living a fulfilled human life. The poverty I am speaking of is rooted in your very existence as a creature of God without whom you cannot exist. In God alone is found true happiness and fulfilment. Are you aware that God alone can satisfy the hungers of your heart? What are the idols that keep you from acknowledging this truth? Are there patterns of disordered possessiveness controlling your life and relationships? It is the desert-hermitage experience that helps to expose these patterns and wean us away from our longing to possess that God may possess us. It is a costly endeavour!

According to Thomas Keating[27] every person awakens to life in this world in a state of consciousness where the focus centres on the fulfilment of physical needs to ensure survival. He maintains that if these needs have been thwarted they may later give rise to inordinate needs for the security symbols of a given culture. When this happens a person constructs a false self, developed and defended on false premises of happiness, supported by emotional programmes to keep them in place.

It may be helpful at this point to look deeply into your heart. What security symbols of your culture (for example: status, money, clothes, possessions, appearances, travel, entertainment) are you attached to and how do you defend them? Do you feel challenged by the teaching of Jesus in the first Beatitude: How blessed are the poor in spirit, the kingdom of Heaven is theirs? If you do feel challenged, what needs to change in your attitudes and in your life right now? What do you understand by 'the kingdom of Heaven'? The kingdom is promised to the poor in spirit and God is faithful to his promises. Do you really believe and trust that God is enough for you? Is your life centred on God who passionately desires to give himself totally to you? Are you ready to accept that your true self, your real identity is discovered in your relationship with him?

Blessed are the gentle. In the context of Psalm 37, the gentle are those who are afflicted in one way or another and yet they are unassuming and undemanding. It is possible to be gentle in the midst of trials and tribulations because God has promised that the gentle shall have the earth for their inheritance. Unlike the first Beatitude, the earth is not yet fully our inheritance but it will be. This will be in God's time and not ours. Therefore, it may be important to address the conscious or unconscious need we have towards power and control. This power and control may be in relation to our own lives, the lives of others, the circumstances in which we find ourselves or the events that mark our ordinary day-to-day existence. This Beatitude invites us to resist the temptation to be in control and to live within the limitations of the human condition which is still very imperfect and in which the wicked actually seem to thrive. But Psalm 37 assures us that it is not so:

> Do not get heated about the wicked
> or envy those who do wrong.
> Quick as the grass they wither,
> fading like the grass of the fields.
>
> Put your trust in Yahweh and do right,
> make your home in the land and live secure.
> Make Yahweh your joy
> and he will give you your heart's desires.
>
> Commit your destiny to Yahweh,
> be confident in him, and he will act. (Ps. 37:1–5)

Jesus was tempted to take control of all the kingdoms of the world. He resisted. His trust was always in God working within the human condition in ordinary limited and provisional ways. How difficult it is for us to allow God to be who he is and form and fashion us in his own image and likeness. Often perhaps, even unwittingly, we try to fashion God in our own image and likeness!

Blessed are those who mourn: they shall be comforted. We do not usually associate blessedness with mourning, so what lies beneath this essential teaching of Jesus? The desert-hermitage experience will purify our hearts and strip us of our ego-driven and selfish desires. This stripping will cause much suffering and grief deep within our hearts and we will mourn the loss of all those aspects of the false self we have constructed to bolster our sense of self. Expect to actually feel the loss. Grief and mourning are emotional states that are heart-rending. Did not the prophet Ezekiel promise that God would remove our stony hearts and give us a heart of flesh instead? Did not Jesus lament hearts that could not feel? St Mark tells us that Jesus was 'grieved at the hardness of heart' of the Pharisees (Mk. 3:5).

Letting go and allowing God to purify us in love will eventually lead to fullness of life and love but it will not be easy. Until we accept the truth of our innate poverty and lovingly accept the reality of our creaturehood, we will continue to strive for what can never be. Mourn the reality of the losses you feel and eventually you will experience the freedom that Jesus promises in this Beatitude: Blessed are those who mourn: they shall be comforted.

Blessed are those who hunger and thirst for uprightness: they shall have their fill. What are the hungers of your heart right now? Are these the hungers of the false self that are boosted by what other people tell you you need in order to be satisfied? Do advertisements or groups to which you belong dictate these needs? How free are you to say 'No' in the events and circumstances that compromise uprightness in your life? Identifying the hungers in your heart is a start to recognizing the deeper motivations of your behaviour. Jesus wants you to be free from the enslavements that tie you to a false sense of who you are. He died that you might live! He passionately desires your freedom in the Holy Spirit. Hunger and thirst for this love and life that Jesus offers. His promise is that you will be filled. Can you take Jesus at his word and really believe this promise?

According to Thomas Keating, the first four Beatitudes correspond to the commandment, 'Love your neighbour as yourself.' They enable us to graduate from our childish programmes once and for all and to move into the freedom to which Jesus invites us. They prepare us for the continuing work of letting go of selfishness and of sensitizing ourselves to the movements of the Spirit, which invite us not only to generous efforts, but also to heroic service of God and other people.[28]

Blessed are the merciful: they shall have mercy shown them. Most Scripture scholars agree that with this Beatitude there is a shift in emphasis. The Gospel is all about love but there is a difference between the command to love others as we love ourselves and to love as Jesus loves us. The latter is much more demanding than the former. Referring to this level of loving, Keating states: 'It is to continue to show love, no matter what the provocation may be to act otherwise.'[29] To love in an ever-deepening, selfless and sacrificial way involves on-going conversion of heart. Such merciful and compassionate love is the hallmark of the all-embracing, all-inclusive and unconditional *hesed* response.

We have already noted that the word *hesed* is commonly associated with mercy. The person with a heart of mercy reaches out to others with a compassionate heart sensitive to human misery and suffering. This blessedness and happiness promised is mercy for oneself. Jesus said: 'They shall have mercy shown them.' How sensitive are you to the misery and suffering of those who touch your life directly within your family circle, friends, neighbours and colleagues? How merciful are you towards yourself and your own failures and shortcomings? Do you find forgiveness of yourself and others difficult? Is there any person from whom you withhold forgiveness and mercy? There is a superabundance of mercy in God that is the foundation for our feeble attempts to forgive and show mercy as we ourselves have received from God.

> Blessed be the God and Father of our Lord Jesus Christ, the merciful Father and the God who gives every possible encouragement; he supports us in every hardship, so that we are able to come to the support of others, in every hardship of theirs because of the encouragement that we ourselves receive from God.
>
> (2 Cor. 1:3–4)

Blessed are the pure in heart: they shall see God. We have already emphasized the place of the heart within the total picture of the Beatitudes. The heart is the deepest centre and source of a person; therefore we cannot overestimate the importance of the biblical understanding, embracing the totality of what it means to be a person. Pope John Paul II, a prolific writer on philosophical, theological and literary themes, develops his insights about the human person in terms of a philosophy of consciousness that is captured in the symbol of the heart.

> In its penetrating analysis of 'the modern world', the Second Vatican Council reached that most important point in the visible world that is man, by penetrating like Christ the depth of human consciousness and by making contact with the inward mystery of man, which in biblical and non-biblical language is expressed by the word 'heart'. Christ, the Redeemer of the world, is the one who penetrated in a unique, unrepeatable way into the mystery of man and entered his 'heart'.[30]

The focus on relationships is crucial in our understanding of the place of the heart and the process of change, as consciousness develops in widening circles of relationships. In this process and development, the desert-hermitage experience is central in identifying the motivations that often lie hidden and keep us bound within narrow circles of selfish loving and living. Having the courage to face the dark corners of our hearts prepares the way for the reshaping that is first and foremost the work of the Holy Spirit. The desert-hermitage experience is important in facilitating the work of purification and conversion, but it is only a means towards the desired end. The desert helps us to co-operate with the Holy Spirit in facing and removing the obstacles to growth and development. Ponder and pray fervently to the Holy Spirit to enlighten, cleanse and purify your heart that you may reflect the beauty that is your unique creation, a work of art in Christ Jesus. 'We are God's work of art, created in Christ Jesus for the good works that God has already designated to make up our way of life' (Eph. 2:9–10).

This inner journey of the heart is the process of becoming in nature and grace what God always intended for humanity. Purity of heart is the restoration of beauty. If we accept this truth we readily become co-creators and co-workers with God for the reign of his Kingdom of Love in our world. Though this beauty is a matter of the heart and its purity and transparency, it is worked out in the everydayness of ordinary life and relationships. It means striving for justice through peace for all our brothers and sisters. This will involve many interior renunciations, the genuineness of which will be known by the fruits, notably the harmony of peace and peacemaking.

Blessed are the peacemakers: they shall be recognized as children of God. This is a costly peace. It involves facing the truth about ourselves that we have already spoken of in the Beatitude of purity of heart. This costly endeavour involves accepting ourselves as we really are with all our beauty and brokenness. If we refuse to accept either our beauty or our brokenness we will not be at peace within ourselves. We will project the one or the other on to other people in an effort to keep the full truth about ourselves at bay. Consciously or unconsciously this pattern in human behaviour prevents us from experiencing the gift of peace that God wishes us to have in Christ.

What aspects of yourself would you rather not face and acknowledge? What characteristics do you find annoying in other people? Could these characteristics be unwanted aspects of you?

What makes you fearful about going deeper into your own heart? Facing the truth of our hidden motivations is never an easy task but once faced, peace has a chance to establish itself in your heart and bless you with the recognition of your true identity. God alone is Truth and he has revealed the truth about your identity: You are a beloved child of God. Nothing and no one can change this reality. Rejoice in this truth about yourself.

Blessed are those who are persecuted in the cause of uprightness: the kingdom of Heaven is theirs. Jesus embraced the role of the Suffering Servant of God and in doing so he endured the persecution that led to his death on the Cross. Speaking with the authority of a close follower who witnessed the cost of discipleship, Peter wrote:

> Christ suffered for you and left an example for you to follow in his steps. He had done nothing wrong, and had spoken no deceit. He was insulted and did not retaliate with insults; when he was suffering he made no threats but put his trust in the upright judge. He was bearing our sins in his own body on the cross, so that we might die to our sins and live for uprightness; through his bruises you have been healed. You had gone astray like sheep but now you have returned to the shepherd and guardian of your souls.
>
> (1 Pet. 2:21–5)

Reflecting on the example of Christ as the patient, Suffering Servant of God, how do you see your daily sufferings, annoyances, trials, tribulations and yes, maybe even persecutions for the stand you take for love of Christ and the values of his Kingdom of Love? Have you considered that you are 'Blessed' because of your patience under very difficult circumstances; especially those sufferings you bear because of your friendship with Christ? To be a Christian is both a privilege and a responsibility. Take time to consider both as you reflect on your life and relationships in the light of this Beatitude.

Embracing the values of the kingdom is the narrow gate through which we pass to fullness of life and love.

> My dear friends, do not be taken aback at the testing by fire which is taking place among you, as though something strange were

happening to you; but in so far as you share in the sufferings of Christ, be glad, so that you may enjoy a much greater gladness when his glory is revealed. If you are insulted for bearing Christ's name, blessed are you, for on you rests the Spirit of God, the Spirit of glory. (1 Pet. 4:12–14)

Invitations to Prayer

Words of Love
1. There is no need to be afraid, little flock, for it has pleased your Father to give you the Kingdom. (Lk. 12:32)
2. Seek first of all the kingdom of God and his justice. (Mt. 6:33)
3. Love one another as I have loved you. (Jn. 15:12)
4. Repent, and believe the Gospel. (Mk. 1:15)
5. Wherever your treasure is, there will your heart be too. (Mt. 6:21)
6. Do not worry about tomorrow. (Mt. 6:34)
7. I tell you, there is rejoicing among the angels of God over one repentant sinner. (Lk. 15:10)
8. The Son of Man has come to seek out what was lost. (Lk. 19:10)
9. My command to you is to love one another. (Jn. 15:17)
10. My grace is enough for you: for power is at full stretch in weakness. (2 Cor. 12:9)
11. God will fulfil all your needs out of the riches of his glory in Christ Jesus. (Phil. 4:19)
12. I will certainly not reject anyone who comes to me. (Jn. 6:37)

Heart Reflections
1. Read Matthew's Gospel, chapter 4 and join Jesus in the desert. Stay with him long enough to enter the deeper regions of your own heart. Talk to him about your inner struggles and then be still and listen.
2. Give time to God today and simply *be* in his company without words, without thoughts, without pretence, without petitions, without resistance, unprotected and vulnerable, open to infinite Love. Linger there.

3. St Gregory the Great said: 'Learn to know the heart of God in the words of God.' Reverently approach Scripture today and seek to know the heart of God. You may wish to choose the Readings the Church suggests for that day, or you may prayerfully wish to read a text of your own choice.

4. The words of Cassian could also serve as an end of the day reflection:

'All the secret places of our heart, therefore, must be constantly scrutinized and the prints of whatever enters them must be investigated in the most careful way.'[31]

Praying with the Psalms

Psalm 51

Have mercy on me, O Gracious One,
according to your steadfast love;
According to your abundant kindness
forgive me where my thoughts and
deeds have hurt others.
Lead me in the paths of justice,
guide my steps on paths of peace!
Teach me, that I may know my weaknesses,
the shortcomings that bind me,
The unloving ways that separate me,
that keep me from recognizing
your life in me;
For, I keep company with fear, and
dwell in the house of ignorance.
Yet, I was brought forth in love,
and love is my birthright.

You have placed your truth in the
inner being;
therefore, teach me the wisdom
of the heart.
Forgive all that binds me in fear,
that I might radiate love;
cleanse me that your light might
shine in me.

Fill me with gladness; help me to
transform weakness into strength.
Look not on my past mistakes
but on the aspirations
of my heart.

Create in me a clean heart, O Gracious One,
and put a new and right spirit
within me.
Enfold me in the arms of love, and
fill me with your Holy Spirit.
Restore in me the joy of your saving grace,
and encourage me with a new spirit.

Then I will teach others your ways,
and prisoners of fear will return
to You.
Deliver me from the addictions of society,
most Gracious One,
O keep me from temptation that
I may tell of your justice
and mercy.

O Gracious One, open my lips and
my mouth shall sing forth
your praise.
For you do not want sacrifice;
You delight in our friendship
with You.
A sacrifice most appropriate is a
humble spirit;
a repentant and contrite heart,
O Merciful One,
is a gift You most desire.

Let the nations turn from war,
and encourage one another as
good neighbours.
O Most Gracious and Compassionate Friend,
melt our hearts of stone,
break through the fears that

lead us into darkness, and
Guide our steps into the way of peace.

Psalm 67
The Beloved is gracious to us
and blesses us;
the radiant One shines upon us.
O, that Love's Way be followed
in all the earth,
Love's saving power among all
the nations.
May the people rejoice in You;
may all people sing with gratitude
to the Beloved!

Let the nations be glad and give
thanks,
for You call the people to
integrity and justice;
You guide the nations upon
the earth.
May the people rejoice in You;
may all the people sing with gratitude
to the Beloved!

The earth yields its harvest;
the Beloved blesses us.
Yes, the Beloved blesses us;
let us abandon ourselves into
the Heart of Love![32]

Praying with St Francis
Almighty, eternal, just and merciful God,
give us miserable ones
the grace to do for You alone
what we know You want us to do
and always to desire what pleases You.
Inwardly cleansed,
interiorly enlightened
and inflamed by the fire of the Holy Spirit,
may we be able to follow

in the footprints of Your beloved Son,
our Lord Jesus Christ,
and, by Your grace alone,
may we make our way to You,
Most High,
Who live and rule
and are glorified
God almighty,
forever and ever.
Amen.[33]

Notes

1. Hopkins, 'My own heart let me more have pity on', in *Poems and Prose*, p. 63.
2. Herbert, 'A True Hymn', in *The Complete Works*, p. 165.
3. Luckman and Kulzer, *Purity of Heart in Early Ascetic and Monastic Literature*, p. 46.
4. Origen, 'The Twelfth Homily', in *Homelies sur Josue*, p. 294.
5. Saint Augustine, *Confessions*, Bk. VIII.10, pp.192–3.
6. 'The Major Legend of St. Francis by St. Bonaventure', in Armstrong *et al.*, *Francis of Assisi*, vol. 2, pp. 531–2.
7. 'The Life of Saint Francis by Thomas of Celano', in Armstrong *et al.*, *Francis of Assisi,* vol. 1, p. 185.
8. Ibid., p. 187.
9. 'The Earlier Rule', in Armstrong *et al.*, *Francis of Assisi*, vol. 1, p. 80.
10 Saint Bonaventure, *Collationes in Hexaemeron*, p. 17.
11. Fox, *A Spirituality Named Compassion*, p. 17.
12. Ibid., p. 23.
13. 'Third Consideration on the Sacred Stigmata', in Habig, *Omnibus of Sources*, p. 1448.
14. Armstrong *et al.*, *Francis of Assisi*, vol. 2, p. 640.
15. 'The Legend of Three Companions', in Armstrong *et al.*, *Francis of Assisi*, vol. 2, p. 108.
16. Cf. Achard of Saint Victor, *Works*, pp. 298–9.
17. Muto, *Blessings That Make Us Be*, p. 118.
18. Van Kaam, *Formation of the Human Heart*, p. 145.
19. Saint Augustine, *Sermons*, Sermon 22A, 4, p. 53.
20. Saint Augustine, Tractate 1.9, in *Tractates on St. John's Gospel*.
21. Saint Augustine, *Confessions*, Bk. IV.11, p. 102.
22. Ibid., Bk. I.5, p. 42
23. Squire, *Asking the Fathers*, p. 107.
24. Saint Ephrem, Hymn VI, in *Hymns on the Nativity*.
25. Saint Augustine, Tractate 1.9, in *Tractates on St. John's Gospel*.
26. Rohr, *Job and the Mystery of Suffering*, pp. 168–71.

27. Keating, *Foundations for Centering Prayer*, p. 244.
28. Ibid., p. 218.
29. Ibid., p. 219.
30. Pope John Paul II, *Redemptoris Hominis*, No. 8, p. 6.
31. Cassian, Conference 1.xxii.i, in *The Conferences*, p. 63.
32. Merrill, *Psalms For Praying*, pp. 99–101, 128.
33. Armstrong *et al.*, *Francis of Assisi*, vol. 1, pp. 120–1.

Chapter 4

Secret of Solitude

CLEANSED, ENLIGHTENED AND PURIFIED, the desert-hermitage experience yields up its secret and enfolds us in its mystery. The great Mystery is the revelation of God as a communion of Love. God is Love and God desires to share this love with us. The Three Persons within the Trinity are one in Love. This life of love within the Trinity is the privilege we are invited to make our own by our sharing in this love. 'My dear friends, let us love each other, since love is from God and everyone who loves is a child of God and knows God. Whoever fails to love does not know God because God is love' (cf.1 Jn. 4:7). We came from the God of Love. This God of Love sustains us in being and our destiny is to be forever within this communion of Love. This astonishing truth is revealed in Scripture. St John reminds us: 'Our life is shared with the Father and with his Son Jesus Christ' (1 Jn. 1:3) and in his second Letter St Peter emphasizes the same remarkable truth: 'The greatest and priceless promises have been lavished on us, that through them you should share the divine nature' (2 Pet. 1:4).

We have already reflected on the purpose of the Incarnation. Jesus came among us as the Beloved Son to share the Father's love with us and to enable us to love him in return. The lovable nature of God draws us into the communion of the Trinity. We are unique creations of God, loved in our uniqueness with the personal love of God who is Father, Son and Holy Spirit. Let us now enter this wonderful Mystery and draw nearer to the Heart of God.

The heart of God

Jesus, the One who is nearest the Father's heart, reminds you now of a precious truth he revealed during his life on earth: 'Everything has been entrusted to me by my Father; and no one knows the Son except the Father, just as no one knows the Father except the Son and those to whom the Son chooses to reveal him' (Mt. 11:27). In his own person, Jesus has made the Father known to you. Linger a little with this wonderful revelation. While on earth, Jesus called God by the familiar term 'Abba', the equivalent of 'Daddy', and he invites you to call God the Father your 'Abba' too. This relationship between Father and Son is the most perfect – beyond our human imaginings. Yet we are called into this relationship in and with and through Jesus.

A slow, faith-filled pondering on the prayer that Jesus taught us might be a starting point for our reflection on God, our 'Abba'. Pray this prayer with Jesus because he did invite us to pray 'Our Father', not 'My Father'. Just as Jesus prays to the Father and gives thanks before receiving his gifts, so he teaches us filial boldness: 'Whatever you ask in prayer, believe that you receive it, and you will.' Such is the power of prayer and of faith that does not doubt: 'all things are possible for him who believes'. Jesus is as saddened by the 'lack of faith' of his own neighbours and the 'little faith' of his own disciples as he is struck with admiration at the great faith of the Roman centurion and the Canaanite woman.[1] Relying heavily on the *Catechism of the Catholic Church*, the following excerpts may help you as you pray and reflect. Later you may wish to reflect and pray with the fuller explanations that are given in the Catechism.[2]

> The Lord's Prayer 'is truly the summary of the whole Gospel'. The prayer that comes to us from Jesus is truly unique. Only Jesus could cross the threshold of the divine holiness and bring us into God's presence. To pray to the Father is to enter into his mystery as he is and as the Son has revealed him to us. The expression 'God the Father' had never been revealed to anyone. We can invoke God as 'Father' because *he is revealed to us* by his Son become man and because his Spirit makes him known to us.

Our Father

When we say 'our' Father, we recognize first that all his promises of love are fulfilled in the *new and eternal covenant* in his Christ: we have become 'his' people and he is henceforth 'our' God. If we pray the *Our Father* sincerely, we leave individualism behind, because the love that we receive frees us from it. If we are to say it truthfully, our divisions and oppositions have to be overcome.

Who Art in Heaven

This biblical expression does not mean a place ('space'), but a way of being; it does not mean that God is distant, but majestic. Our Father is not 'elsewhere': he transcends everything we can conceive of his holiness. The symbol of the heavens refers us back to the mystery of the covenant we are living in when we pray to our Father. He is in heaven, his dwelling place; the Father's house is our homeland. Sin has exiled us from the land of the covenant, but conversion of heart enables us to return to the Father, to heaven.

Hallowed Be Thy Name

Beginning with this first petition to our Father, we are immersed in the innermost mystery of his Godhead and the drama of the salvation of our humanity. Asking the Father that his name be made holy draws us into his plan of loving kindness for the fullness of time. When we say 'hallowed be thy name', we ask that it should be hallowed in us, who are in him; but also in others whom God's grace still awaits.

Thy Kingdom Come

The Kingdom of God has been coming since the Last Supper and, in the Eucharist, it is in our midst. The Kingdom will come in glory when Christ hands it over to his Father. The Kingdom of God is righteousness and peace and joy in the Holy Spirit. This petition is taken up and granted in the prayer *of* Jesus which is present and effective in the Eucharist; it bears its fruit in new life in keeping with the Beatitudes.

Thy Will Be Done on Earth, As It Is in Heaven

Our Father 'desires all men to be saved and come to the knowledge of the truth'. 'He has made known to us the mystery of his will, according to his good pleasure that he set forth in Christ ... to gather up all things in him, things in heaven and things on earth.' We ask insistently for this loving plan to be fully realized on earth as it is already in heaven.

We ask our Father to unite our will to his Son's, in order to fulfil his will, his plan of salvation for the life of the world. We are radically incapable of this, but united with Jesus and with the power of his Holy Spirit, we can surrender our will to him and decide to choose what his Son has always chosen: to do what is pleasing to the Father.

Give Us This Day Our Daily Bread

'Give us': the trust of children who look to their Father for everything is beautiful. Jesus teaches us this petition, because it glorifies our Father by acknowledging how good he is, beyond all goodness.

'Give us' also expresses the covenant. We are his and he is ours, for our sake. But this 'us' also recognizes him as the Father of all and we pray to him for them all, in solidarity with their needs and sufferings.

'Our bread': The Father gives us all appropriate goods and blessings, both material and spiritual. Jesus insists on the filial trust that co-operates with our Father's providence. He is not inviting us to idleness, but wants to relieve us from nagging worry and preoccupation. Such is the filial surrender of the children of God. *'This day'* is also an expression of trust taught us by the Lord, which we would never have presumed to invent.

But the presence of those who hunger because they lack bread opens up another profound meaning of this petition. The drama of hunger in the world calls Christians who pray sincerely to exercise responsibility toward their brethren, both in their personal behaviour and in their solidarity with the human family. In the Beatitudes 'poverty' is the virtue of sharing: it calls us to communicate and share both material and spiritual goods, not by coercion but out of love.

And Forgive Us Our Trespasses, As We Forgive Those Who Trespass Against Us

This petition is astonishing. Our petition begins with a 'confession' of our wretchedness and his mercy. Our hope is firm because, in his Son, we have redemption, the forgiveness of our sins. There is no limit or measure to this essentially divine forgiveness. Now — and this is daunting — this outpouring of mercy cannot penetrate our hearts as long as we have not forgiven those who have trespassed against us. This crucial requirement of the covenant mystery is impossible for man. But 'with God all things are possible'.

And Lead Us Not Into Temptation

This petition goes to the root of the preceding one, for our sins result from our consenting to temptation; we therefore ask our Father not to 'lead' us into temptation. It is difficult to translate the Greek verb used by the single English word: the Greek means both 'do not allow us to enter into temptation' and 'do not let us yield to temptation'. 'God cannot be tempted by evil and he himself tempts no one'; on the contrary, he wants to set us free from evil. We are engaged in the battle 'between flesh and spirit'; this petition implores the Spirit of discernment and strength.

'Lead us not into temptation' implies a *decision of the heart*: 'For where your treasure is, there will your heart be also ... No one can serve two masters.' 'If we live by the Spirit, let us also walk by the Spirit.' In this assent to the Holy Spirit the Father gives us strength. Such a battle and such a victory become possible only through prayer.

But Deliver Us From Evil

In this petition, evil is not an abstraction, but refers to a person, Satan, the Evil One, the angel who opposes God. The devil (*dia-bolus*) is the one who 'throws himself across' God's plan and his work of salvation accomplished in Christ.

Victory over the 'prince of this world' was won once and for all at the hour when Jesus freely gave himself up to death to give us his life. Therefore, the Spirit and the Church pray: 'Come, Lord Jesus', since his coming will deliver us from the Evil One.

When we ask to be delivered from the Evil One, we pray as well to be freed from all evils, present, past and future, of which he is the author or instigator. In this final petition, the Church brings before the Father all the distress of the world. Along with deliverance from the evils that overwhelm humanity, she implores the precious gift of peace and the grace of perseverance in expectation of Christ's return.

Jesus is the only One who can reveal the Father's heart and the Father's divine *hesed*. How else could we know the wonder of such a steadfast, tender, unconditional, compassionate and forgiving love in the heart of the Trinity? And Jesus knew that his mission here on earth was to reveal such stupendous love. 'I have revealed your name to those whom you took from the world to give me. They were yours and you gave them to me' (Jn. 17:6). Loved by the Father from all eternity, you were given to Jesus as a gift so that by his life on earth and his sacrificial, self-giving, self-emptying love on the Cross, you would be re-created and reflect his image and likeness in your own unique way. Your embarking on your heart's journey is your response to the invitation to become whole and integrated; it is the restoration of your beauty as you reflect the glory of God in whose image you are created. This is the Father's will for you. It is a costly love. 'For this is how God loved the world: he gave his only Son' (Jn. 3:16).

The only Son is our Saviour, our Lord, our brother, our teacher, our healer, our Good Shepherd, our dearest friend, our bridegroom and so much more! I am sure you can add to the list yourself as you reflect and converse with Jesus the beloved Son of the Father. There is no doubt about the divine *hesed* in the heart of Jesus. 'I have loved you just as the Father has loved me' (Jn. 15:9). The great mystery of love is that we are free to accept or reject such lavish love. The desert-hermitage experience is one way of facing the reality of such love and realizing the over-whelming truth of the divine *hesed*, so passionately in love with each one of us.

It is the Holy Spirit who leads us into the truth of such love. Alone we could not fathom or face the excess of love with which we are loved. But Jesus promised he would send his Holy Spirit as a gift from the Father. 'The Paraclete, the Holy Spirit, whom the Father will send in my name will teach you everything' (Jn. 14:26). Do you believe that this promise of Jesus is for you? Read the words of Jesus again. Do you sense the wonder of this promise? Do you feel excited and expectant by this promise of Jesus? If you accept the gift of God's Holy Spirit, what are the implications and challenges for you?

Three times Jesus speaks of the Holy Spirit as the Spirit of Truth who issues from the Father and who would remain with us forever and who leads us to the complete Truth. 'I shall ask the Father, and he will give you another Paraclete to be with you forever, the Spirit of Truth' (Jn. 14:16). Later we read: 'When the Paraclete comes, whom I shall send you from the Father, the Spirit of Truth who issues from the Father, he will be my witness' (Jn. 15:26). In another passage Jesus says: 'When the Spirit of Truth comes he will lead you to the complete truth' (Jn. 16:13).

The Holy Spirit will teach you everything. It is the Spirit who will remind you of many words of love that Jesus has already spoken within your heart (cf. Jn. 14:26), and it is the same Holy Spirit who will be your advocate, intercessor, counsellor, protec-tor and support as you continue your heart's journey.[3] Even when you do not know how to pray, St Paul tells us:

> The Spirit too comes to help us in our weakness, for, when we do not know how to pray properly, then the Spirit personally makes our petitions for us in groans that cannot be put into words; and he who can see into all hearts knows what the Spirit means because the prayers that the Spirit makes for all God's holy people are always in accordance with the mind of God. (Rom. 8:26–7)

What a wonderful revelation! To think that the Holy Spirit of God is personally interested in you and me to the extent that he asks the Father for all that brings us healing and wholeness.

St Paul delights in telling us about the life of the Holy Spirit of Love within our hearts. In his beautiful Letter to the Romans St Paul spells out this activity for us. It is the Spirit who prays within us and destroys the reign of sin and the demands of the false self; it is the Spirit who enables us to cry out 'Abba, Father'; it is the Spirit who leads us into freedom, that freedom which is characteristic of a child of God; it is the Spirit who empowers us to rejoice in our destiny of being co-heirs with Christ, sharing his suffering so as to share his glory (cf. Rom. 8). In and through our union with the prayer of the Holy Spirit we will become what God has desired and dreamed for us from all eternity.

You will know if you are responding to the activity of the Holy Spirit within you because again it is St Paul who delights in telling us that when we are guided by the Spirit, the results will be evident: joy, peace, patience, kindness, goodness, trustfulness, gentleness and self-control (cf. Gal. 5:22–4). In other words, when the divine *hesed* is living within our hearts, the human *hesed* response will be evident in our everyday lives and relationships.

In this awesome revelation of the love within the Trinity, the Father has given you his only-begotten Son, and the Son in turn has given you the gift of the Holy Spirit. We live in the world of Gift. We live in the world of Gift because the life of the Three Persons lived within the Blessed Trinity is Gift. Each Person is unceasingly giving the gift of Self to the Other and to you. The divine *hesed* within the Trinity is total and infinite Love, beyond anything we can imagine but so real that we are caught up within this Loving whether we know it or not.

The heart and the hermitage

Believing and adhering to the mystery of the Divine Indwelling, really living within us is the secret of solitude. The awesome reality of the divine *hesed*, pulsing within us, the mystery of One God, Three Persons, Heart of our heart, Life of our life, Love of our love, this is the Gift in which we are embraced. We exist because we are the Life of God's Love, and the journey of the heart leads us to exclaim that Jesus is the Love of our life. This mutuality is a sharing in the overflowing love within the Trinity and it affects forever our seemingly 'ordinary' lives. Radiant with the glory of God, when we live within this circle of love our hearts ache until every person realizes that they and the whole of creation are caught up in this embrace.

The desert-hermitage experience has done its work when we too, like Jesus, thirst for all our brothers and sisters to share in this glimpse of heaven within. There each one will reflect the Incarnate Word in the uniqueness of a single life, lived in utter faith and faithfulness and reaching out to others in compassionate love. This is *hesed*. This is the 'heart-knowledge' promised by the Prophet Hosea in the desert experience. This is the incomprehensible and ineffable mystery that embraces us in our frail humanity.

The heart of Francis

On Mount La Verna St Francis was caught up within the embrace of the Trinity in a way that transformed the totality of his person. Wounded by such passionate and tender love, the heart of Francis melted and the divine *hesed* made of him a living icon of crucified Love. This was the culmination of his heart's journey and that is why it is important for us to ponder his relationship with God within the communion of the Blessed Trinity that we too may learn from him as we continue our journey in faith.

From his grateful heart, Francis exclaimed:

O how glorious it is to have a holy and great Father in heaven! O how holy, consoling to have such a beautiful and wonderful Spouse! O how holy and how loving, gratifying, humbling, peace-giving, sweet, worthy of love, and, above all things, desirable: to have such a Brother and such a Son, our Lord Jesus Christ, Who laid down his life for his sheep and prayed to his Father, saying: *Holy Father, in Your Name save those whom you have given me in the world.*[4]

There is no doubt that Francis had a personal and loving relationship with the Father, the Son and the Holy Spirit. A holy and great Father, a beautiful and wonderful Spouse and a Brother who gave his life for him: this was the intimacy and union Francis enjoyed within the Heart of Trinitarian Love.

How would you describe your relationship with the Father, the Son and the Holy Spirit? Take time to reflect and pray with each Person of the Holy Trinity and be open to new ways of developing your relationship in love, receptivity and response.

St Francis and God the Father

The distinguished Franciscan scholar, Thaddee Matura has written extensively about the loving Father–Son relationship within the Trinity.[5] He specifically mentions three passages from the New Testament that you may wish to ponder and pray: the Priestly Prayer in John 17:1–26; the Prayer in Gethsemane in Matthew 26:36–46 and the Our Father in Matthew 6:9–15. 'These Gospel texts show Jesus standing before his Father in very different circumstances and speaking to him with the assurance of a Son.'[6] According to Matura, these Gospel texts are the foundation for the Office of the Passion[7] written by Francis and then fervently prayed on a daily basis. What are the different circumstances in which you stand before the Father?

When St Francis speaks about God the Father, he uses many words to describe his relationship to him. Already we have seen that he looked upon the Father as holy and great. Numerous times he tells us about the holiness of the Father who is the source and origin of our holiness. Aware of the transcendence of God, Francis uses many words that draw our attention to the Otherness and ineffability of God, but what strikes us most is the heartfelt praise and thanksgiving that fills the heart of Francis in his adoration 'of the Father so holy and so great who revealed himself especially as the loving, tender Father of our Lord Jesus Christ'. Let us listen attentively to the outpouring of Francis' grateful heart.

> All-powerful, most holy,
> Almighty and supreme God,
> *Holy* and just *Father*,
> *Lord* King of *heaven and earth*
> we thank You for Yourself . . .
>
> We thank You
> for as through Your Son You created us,

so through Your holy love
with which You loved us
You brought about His birth
as true God and true man
by the glorious, ever-virgin, most blessed, holy Mary
and You willed to redeem us captives
through His cross and blood and death.[8]

Be attentive to the words Francis uses when addressing God the Father. In his Second Letter to the Faithful, Francis said: 'And day and night let us direct praises and prayers to Him, saying: Our Father, Who art in heaven …'[9] Perhaps you may now wish to pause and with St Francis pray the prayer he wrote which the Lord's Prayer inspired.

O *Our Father* most holy:
Our Creator, Redeemer, Consoler, and Saviour:

Who are in heaven:
In the angels and the saints,
enlightening them to know, for *You, Lord, are Light*;
inflaming them to love, for You, Lord, are love;
dwelling in them and filling them with happiness,
for You, Lord, are Supreme Good, the Eternal Good,
from Whom all good comes
without Whom there is no good.

Holy be Your Name:
May knowledge of You become clearer in us
that we may know
the breadth of Your blessings,
the length of Your promises,
the height of Your majesty,
the depth of Your judgments.

Your Kingdom come:
That You may rule in us through Your grace
and enable us *to come to Your kingdom*
where there is clear vision of You,
perfect love of You,
blessed companionship with You,
eternal enjoyment of You.

Your will be done on earth as in heaven:
That we may love You
with our whole heart by always thinking of you,
with our whole soul by always desiring You,
with our whole mind by always directing all our intentions to You,
and by seeking Your glory in everything,
with all our whole strength by exerting
all our energies and affections of body and soul
in the service of Your love and of nothing else;
and we may love our neighbour as ourselves
by drawing them all to your love with our whole strength,
by rejoicing in the good of others as in our own,
by suffering with others at their misfortunes,
and by giving offense to no one.

Give us this day:
in remembrance, understanding, and reverence
of that love which [our Lord Jesus Christ] had for us
and of those things that He said and did and suffered for us.

Our daily Bread:
Your own beloved Son, our Lord Jesus Christ.

Forgive us our trespasses:
through Your ineffable mercy
through the power of the passion of Your beloved Son
and through the merits and intercession
of the ever blessed Virgin and all Your elect.

As we forgive those who trespass against us:
And what we do not completely forgive,
make us, Lord, forgive completely
that we may truly love our enemies because of You
and we may fervently intercede for them before You,
returning no one evil for evil
and we may strive to help everyone in You.

And lead us not into temptation:
hidden or obvious,
sudden or persistent.

> *But deliver us from evil*:
> past,
> present,
> and to come.
> Glory to the Father, and to the Son, and to the Holy Spirit.
> As it was in the beginning, is now, and will be forever. Amen.[10]

Francis and God the Son

Francis' relationship with the Second Person of the Blessed Trinity, Jesus the Word made flesh, bursts with exuberance, tenderness, love and praise. Let us listen once again to Francis' own words:

> O how holy and how loving, gratifying, humbling, peace-giving, sweet, worthy of love, and, above all things, desirable: to have such a Brother and such a Son, our Lord Jesus Christ, Who laid down His life for His sheep and prayed to His Father, saying: Holy Father, in Your Name save those whom you have given me in the world.[11]

In this text, the relationship of Brother, Son and Shepherd are the focus for Francis' praise, thanksgiving and adoration. There is a richness and depth in Francis' realization and experience of Christ as Brother. If Christ is our Brother then we have a common Father and this is the amazing truth that Christ has revealed to us. He has become one of us and one with us in our frail humanity. This Brother of ours is the One who laid down his life for us and prayed to the Father for our salvation. The heart of Jesus our Brother was on fire with the desire to lead us to the Father and share his Life and Love with us.

Let us listen to Francis in his own words:

> Let us have recourse to Him as *to the Shepherd and Guardian of our souls*, Who says: 'I am the Good Shepherd Who feeds My sheep and I lay down My life for My sheep.' . . . Let us, therefore, hold onto the words, the life, the teaching and the Holy Gospel of Him Who humbled Himself to beg His Father for us and to make His name known.[12]

A Shepherd and a Guardian: let us try to unpack these beautiful images.

Jesus described himself as the Good Shepherd, an image that obviously made a deep impression on St Francis. Speaking of the way in which we are called to imitate Christ, Francis asks us to 'Consider the Good Shepherd Who bore the suffering of the Cross to save His sheep.'[13] In this twenty-first century we may not be as familiar with the image of the Shepherd as were the people of Jesus' time and place yet we cannot miss the truth of the message. Jesus is the Good Shepherd and the Good Shepherd lays down his life for his sheep. We are those sheep. Jesus has laid down his life for you and me. He has saved us from danger and death by putting himself in our place. He knows each one of us by name. He himself has told us so. 'I know my own and my own know me' (Jn. 10:14).

This is an amazing Gospel truth that we have already explored in different ways throughout this book. Yes, each of us is personally known and loved by God, the Father, the Son and the Holy Spirit. Jesus emphasized it by telling the parable of the Lost Sheep. We are told that Jesus searches for the lost *one*. We are not talking about a flock of sheep here, but a lost *one*. And Luke tells us that the Good Shepherd rejoices when he finds the lost one and he returns with it on his shoulders (cf. Lk. 15:4–7). It is this tender, self-sacrificing, self-giving image of the Good Shepherd that appeals to the heart of Francis in following in the footsteps of Christ. Here we see clearly the tenderness of the divine *hesed* in action. Continuing his development of this favourite image, Francis says: 'The Lord's sheep followed Him in tribulation and persecution, in shame and hunger, in weakness and temptation, and in other ways; and for these things they received eternal life from the Lord.'[14]

In your following of Christ and in your relationship with him, how have you experienced the tenderness of the divine *hesed* seeking you out and carrying you back when you have strayed from Love? You may also wish to consider some of the tribulations, persecutions, shame, hunger, weakness and temptations you have endured in your life journey. What other ways have you shared in self-giving, self-sacrificing love that characterizes the *hesed* relationship permeating every aspect of life and love? 'The love of him who loved us greatly, is greatly to be loved!'[15]

Francis and God the Holy Spirit

Love was the heartbeat of Francis' life. Love was the energy and life-force of his heart's journey and his legacy to his followers. Such extravagant, excessive and reckless love Francis learned from the heart of Christ, overflowing with love for his Father and for all his brothers and sisters. The totally lovable nature of God personified in the Holy Spirit filled Francis with a desire for this 'holy activity' of the Spirit of God above all else.[16]

The Holy Spirit is often referred to as the Breath of God – that breath of love between the Father and the Son, life-giving and love-giving Gift to all who become a new creation in Christ. We have already reflected on the many promises Jesus made in relation to the sending and gifting of the Holy Spirit. Francis must have believed and internalized these promises because his whole being was a living desire for this Holy Spirit of God that is his 'holy activity' of love. So many of Francis' writings express the primacy of covenant-love, *hesed*, that enfolds us in the heart of the Trinity and pours itself out in compassionate love for all our brothers and sisters. Let us listen to Francis in his own words:

> *With our whole heart,*
> *our whole soul,*
> *our whole mind,*
> *with our whole strength and fortitude*
> *with our whole understanding*
> with all our powers
> with every effort,
> every affection,
> every feeling,
> every desire and wish
> let us all love *the Lord God*.[17]

Unconditional surrender to the leading of the Holy Spirit of Love in every aspect of loving and living, in every attitude and with all the powers and energy of his being, was the goal of Francis' life.

This is *hesed*, the bond of covenant-love originating in the heart of Trinitarian love and poured into our hearts through the Holy Spirit. St Francis left the world a legacy of love and the perennial challenge is to become love in our own individual and unique way by yielding to the 'holy activity' of the Spirit of God within our hearts. This is his invitation and challenge to you, here and now.

St Francis does not leave you in the dark regarding the signs of the Spirit's activity in your personal life. In fact, he very clearly shows you how to distinguish which Spirit is at work in your life: the Holy Spirit of God or the spirit of sinful flesh. Listen to his words: 'I admonish and exhort the brothers in the Lord Jesus Christ to beware of all pride, vainglory, envy and greed, of care and solicitude for the things of this world, of detraction and murmuring.'[18] This discernment of spirits is further spelled out in The Admonitions of St Francis. These short sayings of Francis are remarkable in their clarity and discernment regarding the spirit that animates our lives and relationships.[19]

In his First Letter to the Faithful, St Francis beautifully and sensitively draws us into the circle of Trinitarian love through the 'holy activity' of the Spirit. He tells us first and foremost that when we love God and one another, the Spirit of the Lord will rest upon us and this same Holy Spirit will make his dwelling place among us. From within this intimacy we are drawn into specific and special relationships with the Trinity. Through this 'holy activity' of the Spirit, we are children of the heavenly Father whose works we do, and we are spouses, brothers and mothers of our Lord Jesus Christ.[20] Really ponder and pray these profound words of St Francis. The implications are awesome. Francis goes on to explain how this wondrous possibility becomes reality:

> We are spouses when the faithful soul is joined by the Holy Spirit to our Lord Jesus Christ. We are brothers to Him when we do *the will of the Father who is in Heaven*. We are mothers when we carry Him in our heart and body through a divine love and a pure and sincere conscience and give birth to Him through a holy activity which must shine as an example before others.[21]

Enveloped in the communion of Love that is the Trinity, we mirror and express this same love in the uniqueness of our personal creation and call. The beauty of our creation and the wonder of our personal call emanate from the depth of our hearts, the dwelling place of God.

Our hearts

Enjoying the intimacy within the communion of the Trinity, Francis invites you to make a dwelling place within your heart for the Divine Mystery of the Trinity. 'Let us always make a home and dwelling place there for Him Who is the Lord God Almighty, Father, Son and Holy Spirit.'[22] Within that dwelling place, Francis urges us to love, honour, adore, praise, bless and glorify the Blessed Trinity who desire to make their home in our hearts.

This 'coming home' is challenging. It involves a journey. A journey into the depths of your own heart, to the core of your being, the seat of your personality, emotions, thoughts and decisions where reality has to be faced for what it really is in the blessedness and brokenness of your truly beautiful and unique life.

In the desert-hermitage experience there is a yearning for healing and wholeness. To be drawn into silence and solitude presupposes a call and invitation by God. The Good Shepherd seeks that which is lost and passionately desires to celebrate your healing and wholeness, your 'coming home' to yourself which is also your 'coming home' to him. He desires to give you life and love in abundance with the lavishness that belongs to him alone. This promise of the fullness of life is given in the context of the Good Shepherd image. Listen to these tender words of Jesus:

> In all truth I tell you,
> I am the gate of the sheepfold.
> All who have come before me
> are thieves and bandits,
> but the sheep took no notice of them.
> I am the gate.
> Anyone who enters through me will be safe:
> such a one will go in and out
> and will find pasture.
> The thief comes

only to steal and kill and destroy.
I have come
so that they may have life
and have it to the full.
I am the good shepherd:
the good shepherd lays down his life for his sheep.
(Jn. 10:7–11)

Life, love, safety, protection, guidance, nourishment, freedom and rejoicing: these are the gifts of the Good Shepherd. Gifts waiting for you in solitude that you may have life and have it to the full. The invitation is to allow you to be found by the Good Shepherd who seeks out and searches for that which is lost within yourself. He alone can bring back those areas of yourself which may have been lost through sin, negligence, or circumstances over which you may or may not have had control – whatever the reason, whatever the circumstances, the invitation *now* is to be found, to be made new, to be made whole. 'I know my own and my own know me' (Jn. 10:14).

Invitations to Prayer

Words of Love
  1. My Darling Child. (Jer. 31:20)
  2. My son/daughter, give me your heart. (Prov. 4:23)
  3. Your Father who sees all that is done in secret will reward you. (Mt. 6:18)
  4. I am telling you not to worry. (Mt. 6:25)
  5. I am the Good Shepherd; I know my own and my own know me. (Jn. 10:14)
  6. I lay down my life for my sheep. (Jn. 10:15)
  7. Holy Father, keep those you have given me true to your name, so that they may be one like us. (Jn. 17:11)
  8. Whoever loves me will be loved by my Father, and I shall love him and reveal myself to him. (Jn. 14:21)
  9. Whoever believes in me will perform the same works as I do myself. (Jn. 14:12)
 10. Father, I want those you have given me to be with me where I am. (Jn. 17:24)

11. Anyone who loves me will keep my word, and my Father will love him, and we shall come to him and make our home in him. (Jn. 14:23)
12. The Spirit of Truth ... he is with you, he is in you. (Jn. 14:17)

Heart Reflections

1. The heart has been described as the place where God manifests himself. Imagine this place and prepare it for Jesus who desires your heart for his home. Where do you need to start? What needs to be done? What attachments clutter your heart? Picture his coming and be ready to welcome him into your home and dwelling place. Now read Matthew 25 and be attentive to his coming in your brothers and sisters today.
2. Jesus says: 'Make my Word your home' (Jn. 8:32). Talk to Jesus about this wonderful invitation and the steps you need to take to make it a reality in your life right now.
3. When St Francis prayed we are told that he 'entreated the Father ... played with the Spouse ... and conversed with the Friend'. Explore these relationships in your own prayer then add other descriptions which are very personal to you.
4. Read John's Gospel, chapter 13. Like St John, rest your heart on the heart of Christ and drink deeply from the secrets of his inmost heart.

Praying with the Psalms

Psalm 132

Enter into the Silence, into the
Heart of Truth;
For herein lies the Great Mystery
where life is ever unfolding;
Herein the Divine Plan is made known,
the Plan all are invited to serve.
Listen for the music of the Holy Word
in the resounding Silence of
the universe.
May balance and harmony be your aim
as you are drawn into the
Heart of Love.

Those who follow the way of Love
with calm and faith-filled
intent,
Know that all is working toward
healing and wholeness.
And may the healing power of love
lift you from the limitations
of fear and ignorance
into the arms of freedom.
May the peace of the Spirit bless
you, and
lead you on life's journey.
Be not afraid of the Silence, for
Wisdom's Voice is heard there!

Psalm 131

Most gracious Presence, let me not
be arrogant,
nor boast of my virtuous deeds;
Let me not seek fame or set my heart
on the riches of the world.
Help me to calm and quiet my soul,
like a child quieted at its
mother's breast;
like a child that is quieted,
be so my soul.
I shall hope in You, O Breath
of my breath,
from this time forth and
forevermore.
Amen. [23]

Praying with St Francis

Prayer and Thanksgiving

Wherever we are,
in every place,
at every hour,
at every time of the day
every day and continually,
let all of us truly and humbly believe,
hold in our heart and love,

honour, adore, serve,
praise and bless,
glorify and exalt,
magnify and give thanks
to the Most High and Supreme Eternal God
Trinity and Unity,
Father, Son and Holy Spirit,
Creator of all,
Saviour of all
Who believe and hope in Him,
and love Him, Who,
without beginning and end,
is unchangeable, invisible,
indescribable, ineffable,
incomprehensible, unfathomable,
blessed, praiseworthy,
glorious, exalted,
sublime and most high,
gentle, lovable, delightful,
and totally desirable above all else
for ever.
Amen.[24]

Notes

1. Cf. *Catechism of the Catholic Church*, p. 556.
2. Cf. ibid., pp. 586–609.
3. *The New Jerusalem Bible*, footnote h, p. 1777.
4. 'Earlier Exhortation (The First Letter to the Faithful)', in Armstrong *et al.*, *Francis of Assisi*, vol. 1, p. 42.
5. Cf. Matura, *Francis of Assisi*, and also 'My Holy Father', pp. 105–31.
6. Ibid., p. 126.
7. 'Office of the Passion', in Armstrong *et al.*, *Francis of Assisi*, vol. 1, pp. 139–57.
8. 'The Earlier Rule', in Armstrong *et al.*, *Francis of Assisi*, vol. 1, pp. 81–2.
9. 'The Later Admonition and Exhortation', in Armstrong *et al.*, *Francis of Assisi*, vol. 1, p. 47.
10. 'A Prayer Inspired by the Our Father', in Armstrong *et al.*, *Francis of Assisi*, vol. 1, pp. 158–60.
11. 'Earlier Exhortation (The First Letter to the Faithful)', in Armstrong *et al.*, *Francis of Assisi*, vol. 1, p. 42.
12. 'The Earlier Rule', in Armstrong *et al.*, *Francis of Assisi*, vol. 1, pp. 80–1.
13. 'Admonition VI', in Armstrong *et al.*, *Francis of Assisi*, vol. 1, p. 131.
14. Ibid.

15. 'The Major Legend of St. Francis by St. Bonaventure', in Armstrong *et al.*, *Francis of Assisi*, vol. 2, p. 596.
16. 'The Later Rule', in Armstrong *et al.*, *Francis of Assisi*, vol. 1, p. 105.
17. 'The Earlier Rule', in Armstrong *et al.*, *Francis of Assisi*, vol. 1, p. 84.
18. 'The Later Rule', in Armstrong *et al.*, *Francis of Assisi*, vol. 1, p. 105.
19. 'The Admonitions', in Armstrong *et al.*, *Francis of Assisi*, vol. 1, pp.128–37.
20. 'The Earlier Exhortation,' in Armstrong *et al.*, *Francis of Assisi*, vol. 1, pp. 41–2.
21. Ibid., p. 42.
22. 'The Earlier Rule', in Armstrong *et al.*, *Francis of Assisi*, vol. 1, p. 80.
23. Merrill, *Psalms for Praying*, pp. 279–80.
24. 'The Earlier Rule', in Armstrong *et al.*, *Francis of Assisi*, vol. 1, pp. 85–6.

Chapter 5

You Know that I Love You

THE DIVINE *HESED* SEEKS a human response. This response is possible because of Jesus. It is in him, the Incarnate Word, that we are called to become our true selves, a word in the Word. In him we discover our identity, our beauty, our goodness, our personal vocation and our mission. That we know this is revealed to us in the words of Jesus himself. At his last meal with his apostles, he prayed to the Father for you and for me, saying:

> Holy Father,
> keep those you have given me true to your name,
> so that they may be one like us.
> While I was with them,
> I kept those you had given me true to your name.
> I have watched over them and not one is lost
> except the one who chose to be lost,
> and this was to fulfil the scriptures.
> But now I am coming to you,
> and I say these things in the world
> to share my joy with them to the full.
> I passed your word on to them,
> and the world hated them,
> because they belong to the world
> no more than I belong to the world.
> I am not asking you to remove them from the world,
> but to protect them from the Evil One.
> They do not belong to the world
> anymore than I belong to the world.
> Consecrate them in the truth;
> Your word is truth. (Jn. 17:11–17)

Jesus prays to his Father for you and for me. Individually we are in his heart and in his prayer. Individually he knows the one who is lost. Individually he has consecrated us in the truth and the truth sets us free; free to live through love in his presence and to express this love in word and deed by the witness of our lives. Jesus desires to have you and me where he is. We know this because he told us so:

> Father,
> I want those you have given me
> to be with me where I am,
> so that they may always see my glory
> which you have given me
> because you loved me
> before the foundation of the world. (Jn. 17:24)

Personally and individually loved within the Life and Love of the Trinity, you are a gift to Jesus from the Father and to enable you to respond and be filled with love, Jesus sent his Holy Spirit to dwell in your heart. You are literally 'one spirit with him' (1 Cor. 6:17). This union in intimacy and love contains within it your personal vocation to share this Trinitarian life with your brothers and sisters. You will do this by living fully your own personal vocation in your own unique way. Your uniqueness is gift. Your uniqueness is precious. Your uniqueness is of God; his image and likeness in you is unrepeatable and eternal. You carry his presence within you in a way that no other person can express and communicate. This is an awesome gift and responsibility. The reality of your personal creation and personal vocation is the secret revealed in the silence and solitude of your own heart. There you will discover not only your own heart but also the heart of God.

The heart of God

We have already reflected on the communion of Love within the Persons of the Blessed Trinity. Here we wish to highlight once again the primacy of love. Love alone rejoices in the beauty of distinctness and difference that the Trinity reveals. The Father is

not the Son and the Holy Spirit is neither the Father nor the Son.
Each is distinct as Persons within the Godhead. Our focus is the
beauty of difference and diversity that emphasizes personal uniqueness and it begins within the Heart of God in a Trinity of Love.

God is Love and within the communion of Love that is the
Trinity, you and I receive life and love as a personal and unique
vocation and mission to become images of God in Christ through
the power of the Holy Spirit. Here we are immersed in a tremendous mystery of extravagant, excessive and lavish love. God
gives. He is the giver par excellence. Not only is the heart of God
extravagant, excessive, lavish and the giver par excellence; God
is a humble Servant-God whose self-giving in love is total, unconditional, infinite and definitive. This love is offered to each and
every individual in a personal, loving relationship with the utter
selfless generosity and sensitivity that gives with the freedom to
accept or reject the gift.

The heart and the hermitage

Immersed in the mystery of God's personal love for you, the
silence and solitude of the hermitage may be for you, as for many
people before you, the chosen place of your response to this love.
From all eternity God has a dream for you and for your life. At
this stage of your heart's journey, the hermitage provides that
sacred space that helps you to delve deeper into the reality of who
you are, where you have come from, why you are here and where
you are going. It is another way of engaging in the big questions
of life, of your particular life: your origin, your purpose and your
destiny. The awesome reality is that right here and now you have
a choice, the freedom to choose whether or not you will take
responsibility for your God-given creation with its unique
personal vocation and mission.

Within the depths of his heart and in the silence and solitude of
the hermitage, St Francis learned his own essential truth and at
the end of his life he exclaimed: 'I have done what is mine; may
Christ teach you what is yours.'[1] Let us learn from St Francis and
allow our hearts to discover the uniqueness of our own creation,
call and mission.

The heart of Francis

'The Lord told me what He wanted.'[2] These words of St Francis
reveal his personal conviction of his personal call by God. They
were spoken at the little chapel of the Portiuncula during a
General Chapter in the presence of the Bishop of Ostia and five
thousand brothers. At a time when others were trying to influence Francis to walk a different way, he had the personal conviction of his personal vocation.

In his Testament, Francis again emphasizes the personal call
and initiative of God: 'And after the Lord gave me brothers, no
one showed me what I had to do, but the Most High Himself
revealed to me that I should live according to the pattern of the
Holy Gospel.'[3] You and I may feel that Francis was one of a rare
and privileged class whose personal vocation was a special revelation by God and we may not feel that we are in this category. A
closer examination of the facts and dynamics involved may help us
to see both the call of Francis and our own call very differently.
Are we not all called to live according to the pattern of the holy
Gospel? The way we come to this realization and the unique way
in which we express this reality will be different for each of us but
there will always be similarities in the pattern of the call and
response. Though we have reflected on many of the events in the
life of Francis, we will now focus attention on the way in which a
personal vocation is gradually discovered and the ways in which it
is lived at ever greater depth.

If we go back to Francis' earlier years, we see a young man
struggling with fame and fortune, power and prestige, war and
peace, family and friends in much the same way that affects any
young person seeking their identity and fulfilment in life. His
personal search led him down many roads of discovery that
brought him no peace, much disillusionment, pain and suffering.
Literally, the world of Francis fell apart until he discovered his
true and personal vocation in life. It was not an easy journey for
Francis and it will not be easy for you and me. What is significant
is that Francis was a man with dreams and desires. Oh yes, these
dreams and desires may have side-tracked Francis' real vocation
in life for a time, but Scripture reminds us that for those who love

God everything works together for their good (cf. Rom. 8:23).

The search for the 'true self' made in the image and likeness of God is the foundation of the heart's journey. It is a process that continues through life. Our dreams and desires may help us to recognize the directions to take and to avoid if we wish to persevere in the adventure. So it was for Francis. He had a dream. The dream was one that thrilled his heart because of the promise of worldly fame, prosperity and popularity. His dream was one of a beautiful palace with a lovely bride and surrounding him were the reminders of military achievements. But very soon afterwards, when Francis was already on his journey to make this dream a reality, he had another dream.

The second dream challenged him deep within his heart as the voice of the Lord questioned his direction and motivation. Significantly, Francis asks the perennial question that faces each of us on the journey of life: 'Lord, what do You want me to do?' The Lord answered: 'Go back to the land of your birth because I will fulfil your dream in a spiritual way.'[4] We are told that Francis turned back without delay. These dreams are very important because they keep alive Francis' search for meaning in his life. At each step of the way, God takes Francis where he is and leads him onwards and inwards. God will do the same for you. Once again reflect on your dreams and desires. How has God led you step by step through disillusionment, failure, meanderings, and new beginnings, until this present moment? What is your heart's desire and your dearest dream right now?

Following on from the realm of dreams, we will now reflect on a few key experiences in the life of Francis. These experiences may help you on your heart's journey as you seek to know, embrace and deepen your understanding of your personal call, vocation and mission in life. Let us look briefly at a few of the calls in the life of St Francis because call and response are gradual steps that lead to personal identity and wholeness.

After the dream episodes, perhaps the most well-known call of Francis is the one that happened in the little church of San Damiano. Disillusioned by his dream of knighthood and the honours of this world, Francis, wearied with his search for meaning in his life yet persevering for that elusive 'something more' wandered into the little broken-down church and, moved by the Holy Spirit, prayed for enlightenment of heart. His prayer was answered with a definite and personal invitation from the Crucified Christ on the Cross: 'Francis, go and repair my house which, as you see, is all being destroyed.'[5]

We are told that Francis was trembling and stunned by this experience and that he absorbed the power of the divine words into his heart and prepared himself to obey and carry out this command. Call and response. They occur and recur in every person's life whether they are recognized or not. You too have heard the divine words in Scripture. You too have absorbed the power of the inspired words of Scripture in your heart and then like Francis, filled with joy you have resolved to obey and carry out the command of the Lord, not once but over and over again. Already you have reflected and prayed on many images and words of love from sacred Scripture. What images and words have made a most lasting impression in your heart? These images and words may give you further insights into your own personal vocation, a vocation that is unrepeatable and unique.

Scripture tells us that each of us is 'called by name'. We have numerous instances of such personal calling by name: Abraham, Moses, Isaiah, Jeremiah, Paul, Mary, the Apostles and so many more. This is the pattern of God's dealings with us. It is always personal, always unique. Francis too was called by name as he prayed in the little church of San Damiano. In that experience Francis encountered the excessive and personal love with which he was loved and he found his unique and true 'self' as he responded to the self-giving of the God of crucified love, who humbled himself and emptied himself in self-giving love. Francis strove to do the same. The divine *hesed* in the heart of God, manifested in poverty and humility found a resonance in the heart of Francis. Compassionate love led him to desire total identification with the poor, humble and crucified Christ.

What began in that little church of San Damiano was deepened as Francis continued to respond to successive calls where the Cross was central. He was challenged to see the poor and suffering Christ, not only on the Cross but also in the bodies of his suffering brothers and sisters, especially in the outcast of the

society of his day, the lepers. St Bonaventure links Francis'
service to the lepers with his experience of Christ Crucified. We
are told that Francis met a leper and the sight of the leper filled
him with horror. However, Francis was determined to conquer
himself. He descended from his horse and, with compassionate
love, gave the man money and a kiss. When he remounted and
looked back, he could not see the leper anywhere. He had
embraced the Crucified in the form of the leper and he was filled
with wonder and joy.[6]

That this was a key moment of call and response in the life of
Francis is confirmed by Francis himself in his Testament:

> The Lord gave me, Brother Francis, thus to begin doing penance
> in this way: for when I was in sin, it seemed too bitter for me to
> see lepers. And the Lord Himself led me among them and *I showed
> mercy* to them.[7]

Francis showed mercy to them. Mercy is one of the most
favoured words associated with *hesed*. Francis was moved by *hesed*
and in responding he deepened his personal vocation in becoming
a living expression of compassionate love.

The call to become a Gospel person in imitation of Christ led
Francis to a continued and attentive listening to the Word of God.
What he heard in the depths of his heart, he put into practice in
his life. In such attentive listening and acting, Francis further
discovered his unique call and exclaimed: 'This is what I want;
this is what I seek, this is what I desire with all my heart.'[8] When
you hear or read sacred Scripture, is this your response? Which
images or words set your heart on fire with desire? In time, you
may notice a pattern in your response to certain words and
images and this is very significant because your unique and very
personal vocation is there, waiting to be revealed, waiting for
your response.

Towards the end of his life St Francis spent forty days in the
hermitage on Mount La Verna. During that period on 14 September
1224 on the Feast of the Exaltation of the Cross, Francis prayed:

> O my Lord Jesus Christ, two graces do I pray thee to grant unto
> me before I die: the first, that while I live I may feel in my body

and in my soul, so far as is possible, that sorrow, sweet Lord, that
thou didst suffer in the hour of thy most bitter passion; the
second, that I may feel in my heart, as far as may be possible, the
exceeding love wherewith, O Son of God, thou wast enkindled to
endure willingly for us sinners agony so great.[9]

At the outset of his heart's journey, Francis was mysteriously
drawn by the attraction and force of crucified Love. Here at the
end of his life, it reaches a climax and through his response to his
initial attraction – his personal vocation – Francis is totally transformed into that which he loves. The heart of Francis and the
heart of Christ were one. Solitude had produced in Francis that
total transformation whereby his whole person was one with
Christ. The wounds of the Crucified Christ were imprinted on
the body of Francis. Almost immediately after this momentous
and mystical encounter Francis, moved with compassion, burned
with zeal to preach and show mercy. *Hesed*, heart and hermitage
had done their work but the way in which they interrelate is
unique within each person.

Our hearts

The Jesuit priest, Herbert Alphonso, writes very convincingly
about Personal Vocation. He equates the biblical 'calling by
name' as the deepest self, with God-given uniqueness that he calls
'Personal Vocation'.[10] Alphonso goes on to develop this beautiful
reality of personal vocation and suggests that it is the secret of
unity and integration at the heart of life and in so doing he stresses
the central place of the Word of God.

St Paul reminds us that the Word of God is alive and active. In
discovering and deepening your sense of who you are, the words of
Scripture are very important. Engage with the Word of God and
eventually you too, like St Francis will become a Gospel person.
Let me take you back to one event in the life of St Francis that may
help you in your search for your personal vocation. According to
his biographer, St Bonaventure, it happened like this:

> In the church of the Virgin Mother of God,
>   her servant Francis *lingered*
>   and, with continuing cries,
>   insistently begged her
>   who had conceived and brought to birth
>   *the Word full of grace and truth,*
>   to become his advocate.
>   Through the merits of the Mother of Mercy,
>   he conceived and brought to birth
>   the spirit of the Gospel truth.

> One day while he was devoutly hearing a Mass of the Apostles, the Gospel was read in which Christ sends out his disciples to preach and gives them the Gospel form of life, that they *may not keep gold or silver or money in their belts, nor have a wallet for their journey, nor may they have two tunics, nor shoes, nor staff.* Hearing, understanding, and committing this to memory, this friend of apostolic poverty was then overwhelmed with an indescribable joy. 'This is what I want,' he said, 'this is what I desire with all my heart!'[11]

Notice the sequence of events. There is a deliberate placing of oneself in a sacred space, for example a church, a hermitage, or other sacred space set apart for prayer. Our Lady, the Mother of God, the one who pondered the Word in her heart and conceived the Word in her body, was asked to be an intercessor. There followed a proclamation of the Word and an attentive listening to it. In responding to the Word, the life of Francis was changed forever. The congregation present at Mass that February morning heard the same Gospel yet one man's heart was touched so deeply that he heard it as a personal word and a personal call. And he acted upon it in such a way that his life was changed forever, and not only his life but also the life of the Church and the world, not just then but to the present day.

In summary we could say that first we have to create the dispositions for prayer by choosing our place and our time. The second step is entering into a personal relationship with the Lord and/or with Mary, God's Mother and ours, by voicing our desires and sharing our dreams. The third step is listening. This may be the hardest of all – especially for some people. The fourth step is receiving the Word within our hearts in a deeply personal way. Finally there is a very definite response. When we allow the Word of God to take flesh within us, to come to birth within us, then something wonderful happens. Mysteriously and in faith, we get in touch with our uniqueness through the word or words that are 'spirit and life' for us.

Perhaps another personal example of the way this can happen might be insightful for you. I share my own experience. Before I became a Sister in a Religious Congregation, I was browsing through the Religion section in a public library near my home. I was discerning my own vocation in life and I was particularly interested in the way in which God calls different people to different vocations; and even within chosen states of life, each one lives the vocation differently, that is personally and in a unique and unrepeatable way.

As I browsed, three words, 'Bride of Christ', touched my heart in such a way that I knew deep within me who God was for me and how he was inviting me to deepen my personal relationship with him. This was confirmed for me when I received St Agnes as my Patron for Religious Life. In the liturgical texts for the Feast of Agnes, virgin and martyr, we read in the Antiphons for Morning Prayer:

> My Lord, Jesus Christ, has placed a ring on my finger; he has adorned me like a bride with a crown.

> He who is the Lord of the angels is the one to whom I am betrothed. The sun and the moon reflect his beauty.[12]

These three words 'Bride of Christ' are still as alive to me now as they were then. The relationship of 'spouse' is deeply rooted in both the Old and New Testaments, in liturgical texts and in the writings of the mystics to describe a person's intimacy with God. Through my studies in biblical and mystical theology, my insights into the depth and richness of spousal spirituality have deepened and changed through the years but always in the context of the original words. A passage from the prophet Hosea that I quoted at the beginning of this book had particular relevance for me in developing the quality of the spousal relationship, but for me this was developed in the context of *hesed*, heart and hermitage.

The whole concept and reality of spousal love is a tremendously demanding and challenging one. It presupposes a union with the Beloved not only in joy and happiness but also in poverty, humility and crucified love that is inherent in the process of transformation and in the unconditional and self-giving service to one's brothers and sisters. Such commitment and fidelity to covenant-love is rooted in the *hesed* relationship, both divine and human. The desired intimacy and union presupposed in spousal love is not special to consecrated religious. No, it is the call of every Christian, man and woman, to enter into the life and mission of the Word made flesh, Jesus Christ, in a love that is on the one hand passionately personal and exclusive, and on the other hand is all-embracing and inclusive. The depth and quality of our personal relationship with the Word made flesh, Jesus Christ, also determines the depth and quality of our relationships with our brothers and sisters and with the whole of creation. The two great commandments – love of God and love of others – are inseparable. The love and intimacy of the spousal relationship will be fruitful in loving service within our own particular circumstances and state of life, as we bring Christ to birth in ourselves and in our world.

In the Franciscan tradition, especially in the lives of St Francis and St Clare, spousal love is no mere romantic or sentimental notion but an invitation to enter more deeply into the total self-giving in love in union with Jesus, the Beloved. We will let St Francis and St Clare speak for themselves as they invite you to deepen your prayer in spousal love. In her Second Letter to Agnes of Prague, Clare writes:

> Your Spouse, though *more beautiful than the children of men* (Ps. 44:3), became, for your salvation, the lowest of men, was despised, struck, scourged untold times throughout His entire body, and then died amid the suffering of the Cross.
>
> O most noble Queen,
> gaze upon Him,
> consider Him,
> contemplate Him
> as you desire to imitate Him.[13]

This gaze leading to imitation is not inward-looking but intensifies Clare's desire to participate fully in the life and mission of her
Spouse. In her Third Letter to Agnes of Prague she says, 'I
consider you a co-worker of God Himself [cf. 1 Cor. 3:9; Rm.
16:3] and a support of the weak members of His ineffable
Body.'[14]

Francis, in his Second Letter to the Faithful, writes in deeply
relational language and like Clare, he too reminds us of the nature
and call of true spousal love: spiritual motherhood in giving birth
to Christ. How are we to do this? Francis says:

> We are spouses when the faithful soul is joined by the Holy Spirit
> to our Lord Jesus Christ. We are brothers, moreover, when we
> do *the will of* His *Father Who is in heaven*; mothers when we carry
> Him in our heart and body through love and a pure and sincere
> conscience; and give Him birth through a holy activity, which
> must shine before others by example ... O how holy, consoling
> to have such a beautiful and wonderful Spouse![15]

How wonderfully God deals with each one of us! Hearing the
words 'Bride of Christ' deep within my heart gave meaning to my
life and my vocation in life. These words also revealed to me what
Fr Alphonso describes as my 'face' of God. In other words, the
way in which God revealed himself to me was unique to me and
to my call and response. In a mysterious way these words reveal
to me who I am becoming in Christ.

At the time when the words 'Bride of Christ' seemed to jump
off the page for me, I knew every person is called to a vocation in
life but I did not understand the term personal vocation in the
sense that I now understand it. Such a discovery of personal identity in Christ is described by Fr Alphonso as 'the central nucleus
of a rich personal synthesis for life and ministry'.[16]

The Word that brings you into being makes you the unique
person you are. Taking into account the blend of your personal
gifts, qualities, talents, skills, aptitudes, character and personality, you will discover the thrill of becoming the person you are
called to be. You and no other! As St James reminds us: 'By his
own choice he gave birth to us by the message of the truth that we
should be a kind of first fruits of his creation' (Jm. 1:18).

Believe with all your heart that a Word of Truth brings us to birth from the Father. What is your Word? What is that special Word that makes you a kind of first fruits? In a pontifical document entitled *New Vocations for a New Europe* there is great emphasis on the vocation of every person.

> The human being, in fact, is 'called' to life, and how he comes to life, carries and finds in itself the image of He who called him. Vocation is the divine invitation to self-realization according to this image, and is unique-singular-unrepeatable precisely because this image is inexhaustible. Every creature expresses and is called to express a particular aspect of the thought of God. There he finds his name and his identity; he affirms and ensures his freedom and originality.[17]

Significantly, and in the context of our particular reflections throughout this book, the above document emphasizes Love as the vocation of every person.

> Love is the full meaning of life. God has so loved man as to give him his very life and to make him capable of living and loving in the divine manner. In this excess of love, the original love, man finds his radical vocation, which is a 'holy vocation' (2 Tim. 1:9), and discovers his own unique identity, which immediately makes him similar to God 'in the image of the holy One' who called him (1 Pet. 1:15). In every person, no-one excluded, there is an original gift of God which waits to be discovered.[18]

I hope you too will discover your original gift in the experience of union with a word or a number of words that reveal the dream God has for you. May it become for you true heart-knowledge leading you to the fullness of life and love in a vocation that is personal, unique and unrepeatable.

Jesus, the Only Begotten and Beloved Son of the Father is the First-born and the First fruit. He is the totality of the Word made flesh. But, you and I find our uniqueness and our identity in him because the Person of Jesus Christ is so infinitely rich that he embraces all calls and all vocations.[19]

> Objectively speaking, no call comes from God to any person

except in the person of Christ Jesus; and no person makes a
response to God's call except in the person of Christ Jesus. This
is the only way of expressing the fundamental biblical truth of
Christ's unique mediation: 'There is one God, and there is one
mediator between God and men, the man Christ Jesus.'

(1 Tim. 2:5)[20]

If and when you get in touch with your personal Word it will have
a way of transforming everything else in your life because you will
have meaning and purpose that will be life-giving, energizing and
fulfilling in a way that nothing else can be. Whether you are
aware or not of your own uniqueness within the creative *hesed* of
God, your very personal relationship with Christ Jesus came to
birth in a special way at baptism. In his Letter to the Romans St
Paul suggests that we are plunged into the Christ Mystery and
clothed with Christ in a unique and personal way (Rom. 6:3).
Again it is Paul who tells us that God's plan for each of us is to be
conformed to the Image of his Son (cf. Rom. 8:29), and in
Ephesians we are encouraged to strive for maturity in Christ Jesus
(Eph. 4:13). Each of us longs for the maturity that brings healing
and wholeness into our lives.

We have already said that Jesus is the human Face of God. The
question and the challenge for you now is to express the Face of
Jesus for your brothers and sisters! The discovery of your
personal vocation will be the key to living this awesome mystery.
Let me tell you a story from the life of St Francis that illustrates
the beautiful truth of personal uniqueness.

Describing his brotherhood, Francis used to highlight the
specific Face of God that he saw in his brothers. They were all
different but each one was very important in expressing the fullness of Christ. He praised the faith and love and poverty of
Brother Bernard, the simplicity and purity of Brother Leo, the
courtesy and kindness of Brother Angelo, the friendly manner
and common sense of Brother Masseo, the contemplation of
Brother Giles, the constant prayer of Brother Rufino, the
patience of Brother Juniper, the spiritual strength of Brother
John of Lauds, the charity of Brother Roger, the solicitude, care
and concern of Brother Lucidus. Each of these brothers made
Jesus present in a personal and unique way that reached out to

others in the practical living of ordinary everyday circumstances.

No one person can express the fullness of Christ but together we are the Body of Christ. In responding to his or her personal vocation each will be formed in his image. 'The history of every person is a little story, but is always a unique part of a greater story.'[21] Rejoice that you have been chosen in Christ 'to live through love in his presence' (cf. Eph 1:4). This brings us back to *hesed*, heart and hermitage: once again we see their inter-relatedness in discovering personal uniqueness, vocation and mission.

Hesed, the divine creative activity within God, calls you into being in love, unique and distinct from every other creation of God, gifting you with your very own way of incarnating God in your human life and relationships and affecting every aspect of your personhood: your heart. We have already noted that in biblical terms the heart is the sum total of who you are as a person. Your heart is your innermost core, the realm where mystery, paradox, freedom and grace meet. The desert-hermitage experience, in whatever form it takes in a person's life, is often the privileged place of revelation. If this is true for you, then it is also true for every other person who has ever lived, is living or will live in the future. Think of the consequences of this truth and wonder at the mystery of it.

If every person is a unique creation of God's love, then the Face of God is revealed within every human being. Every person is for you a manifestation of God, an icon of God! Jesus reminded us of this mysterious reality in many of his teachings, the best known of which is probably the account of the Last Judgement in Matthew's Gospel. Let us meditate on this passage and allow the truth of the message to enter deeply into our hearts and be reflected in our lives.

> When the Son of man comes in his glory, escorted by all the angels, then he will take his seat on the throne of glory. All nations will be assembled before him and he will separate people one from another as the shepherd separates sheep from goats. He will place the sheep on his right hand and the goats on his left. Then the King will say to those on his right hand, 'Come, you whom my Father has blessed, take as your heritage the kingdom prepared for you since the foundation of the world. For I was

hungry and you gave me food, I was thirsty and you gave me
drink, I was a stranger and you made me welcome, lacking
clothes and you clothed me, sick and you visited me, in prison and
you came to see me.' Then the upright will say to him in reply,
'Lord, when did we see you hungry and feed you, or thirsty and
give you drink? When did we see you a stranger and make you
welcome, lacking clothes and clothe you? When did we find you
sick or in prison and go to see you?' And the King will answer, 'In
truth I tell you, in so far as you did this to one of the least of these
brothers of mine, you did it to me.' (Mt. 25:31–40)

The first followers of Jesus seem to have grasped this message in
its depth because in the First Letter of St John we read: 'Anyone
who says: "I love God" and hates his brother, is a liar, since no one
who fails to love the brother whom he can see can love God
whom he has not seen' (1 Jn. 4:20). The love of God and love for
others go hand in hand because as St John says: 'God is Love' (1
Jn. 4:8). 'Life is the masterpiece of the creative love of God and
is in itself a call to love.'[22] We live within and share this love, the
very being of God, 'in whom we live and move and have our
being' as St Paul so aptly states.

In the context of the biblical, Christian and Franciscan tradition, the desert or hermitage is the opportune place to continue
the universal quest for the fullness of love which is mysteriously
contained in the twofold but unified experience of contemplation
and compassion. This is the integration of Martha and Mary (cf.
Lk. 10:38–42) in our lives. Love alone unifies and integrates.
Whether the work of Martha or the prayer of Mary, the goal is the
same: love. If this is missing, then both work and prayer are ends
in themselves and neither further the reign of God or bring fulfilment to the human heart.

We have already reflected on Jesus, who gave his life for each
one of us. He gave his life because he loves us. We too are called
to lay down our lives and according to our unique and personal
vocation, this may take many forms. Whether love is expressed in
service or in prayer, modelled on the life of Martha or of Mary,
the contemplative stance of Mary's attentiveness to the Word and
Martha's loving service to her brothers and sisters are pivotal.
Mary, attentive to the Word, is symbolic of spousal intimacy.

Martha, active in loving service is symbolic of spiritual fecundity or spiritual motherhood. Therefore, the dispositions of the heart and the place of the desert-hermitage in the heart's conversion and transformation are central within the biblical, Christian and Franciscan tradition.

Love of God and love of neighbour lie at the heart of the *Shema* (cf. Deut. 6:4ff.) which embraces the biblical concept of *hesed* and covenant. Love is central and love alone lasts forever. We are immersed in the Love that is God and at some stage in your heart's journey, possibly in the silence and solitude of the hermitage, where you have responded to the invitation of Jesus to 'Come away to some lonely place all by yourself and rest for a while' (Mk. 6:31), you too will be faced with the question that can only be answered by you. In this affair of the heart, no one else can make this answer for you. It is the same personal question that Jesus asked St Peter on the shores of Galilee: 'Do you love me?' (Jn. 21:15ff.). Like St Peter, may your response be as total and unconditional as his: 'Lord, you know everything; you know I love you.'

Invitations to Prayer

Words of Love
1. He chose us in Christ before the world was made. (Eph. 1:3)
2. He has let us know the mystery of his purpose, according to his good pleasure which he determined beforehand in Christ. (Eph. 1:9)
3. There are many different gifts, but it is always the same Spirit; there are many different ways of serving, but it is always the same Lord. (1 Cor. 12:4–5)
4. Now Christ's body is yourselves, each of you with a part to play in the whole. (1 Cor. 12:27)
5. Make love your aim. (1 Cor. 14:1)
6. The particular manifestation of the Spirit granted to each one is to be used for the general good. (1 Cor. 12:7)
7. The love of Christ overwhelms us. (2 Cor. 5:14)
8. All of us, with our unveiled faces like mirrors reflecting the glory of the Lord, are being transformed into the image that we reflect. (2 Cor. 3:18)

9. It is plain that you are a letter from Christ. (2 Cor. 3:3)
10. Your new birth was not from any perishable seed but from imperishable seed, the living and enduring Word of God. (1 Pet. 1:23)
11. By his own choice he gave birth to us by the message of the truth so that we should be a sort of first fruits of all his creation. (Jm.1:18)
12. Do you love me? (Jn. 21:17)

Heart Reflections
1. The Word became flesh in the womb of Mary. Spend some time with Mary and reflect on the dignity, wonder and uniqueness of your creation. What aspects of your humanity do you feel most comfortable/uncomfortable with? Be open to whatever Mary, your Mother, wishes to reveal to you.
2. You are called by God to become a unique creation in Christ. In becoming an 'incarnation of the Incarnation' what text of sacred Scripture do you express or desire to express through your life as your very own 'personal vocation'?
3. Reflect on the story of Martha and Mary (Luke 10:38–42). Be present with Jesus, Martha and Mary. Do you identify with Martha or with Mary? Why? Explore your feelings and attitudes as you reflect on this story. What challenges you most in Martha? In Mary? Write down your reflections.
4. Read the Testament of St Francis.[23] With a heart full of praise and thanksgiving, write your own Testament.

Praying with the Psalms

Psalm 143
O Bringer of Joy, awaken my heart;
pour your love and blessings
through all my being!
Free me from attachments and desire,
that I may become a clear mirror,
reflecting your love to
the world.

For fear has pursued me, it has
crushed my spirit to
the ground;
it has veiled your light so
that I dwell in darkness.
Therefore, I cry out to You,
O Great Awakener;
Help me to rise once again
like the phoenix of old!

I recall days gone by; I meditate
on all that You have done;
I muse on the Covenant of
your love.
I open my heart to You;
my soul thirsts for You like
a parched land.

Strength comes with pureness of heart.
Cleanse me anew, O Gentle Healer.
This yearning within my soul is
naught but the inner birthright
to know and live in You.
Let me hear your Voice within the Silence,
for in You I put my trust.
Teach me ways of loving service,
that I might co-operate with You,
O my Beloved.

Help me to face my fears,
O Divine Nurturer!
I call on You for healing!
Instruct me in your Divine Precepts,
cultivate my soul!
Lead me into deep silence and
solitude,
let peace become my mantle.

Divine Light shines in those
whose lives reflect love.
As the river makes its way to

the ocean,
may I surrender to the flow
of new life!
Then will I trust that all is
working together toward the
wholeness of humanity.
Then will I help to rebuild the
soul of the world with Love!

Psalm 72
Bring justice to the peoples,
O Beloved,
and your mercy to all
generations!
May the people be known for
mercy,
rendering justice to the poor!
Let their spirits soar as the eagle
let joy abide in every heart!
May You heed the cry of the poor –
the young and the old,
setting free all those in need,
melting the heart of the oppressors!

May we know You as long as the sun
endures,
and as long as the moon,
throughout all generations!
May we acknowledge You in the rain
falling on the fields,
like showers that water the earth!
In our day may justice flourish,
and peace abound,
throughout all the nations!

May every heart open to your love
from sea to sea,
from the River of Life out
to the universe!
May fears that imprison the people
be brought to the Light,

and rise from the depths!
May the leaders of nations from
all the earth,
listen to your Word;
May they spend time in Silence
before they counsel!
May the leaders surrender to
your love, and
the nations serve the Most High!

For You heed the needy when
they call,
the poor and those who have
no friend.
You have compassion on the weak,
the downtrodden,
and give them strength and
hope,
From injustice and oppression,
You redeem their life;
and precious are they in
your Heart.

Long may You live in our hearts,
may praises be sung to You!
May our prayers rise up before You
and blessings of love be
freely rendered!
May we be ever grateful for the
grain of the fields,
for the fruits of the vine
to be shared with all;
And may the people blossom forth
in the cities,
like flowers in the meadow!

May your Name live on forever,
your Love endure as long as
the sun!
May the people bless themselves
by You, and

all nations call You blessed!
Blessed be the Beloved, the One
who dwells in open hearts,
who guides us along the way.
Blessed be You, who come in
Name of Love;
may your glory fill the earth!
Amen and Amen![24]

Praying with St Francis

Let every creature
in heaven, on earth, in the sea and in the depths,
give praise, glory, honour and blessing
To Him Who suffered so much,
Who has given and will give in the future every good,
for He is our power and strength,
Who alone is good,
Who alone is almighty,
Who alone is omnipotent, wonderful, glorious
and Who alone is holy,
through endless ages.
Amen.[25]

Notes

1. Armstrong *et al.*, *Francis of Assisi*, vol. 2, p. 386.
2. Armstrong *et al.*, *Francis of Assisi*, vol. 3, p. 314.
3. Armstrong *et al.*, *Francis of Assisi*, vol. 1, p. 125.
4. Armstrong *et al.*, *Francis of Assisi*, vol. 2, p. 245.
5. Armstrong *et al.*, *Francis of Assisi*, vol. 2, p. 536.
6. Armstrong *et al.*, *Francis of Assisi*, vol. 2, p. 534.
7. Armstrong *et al.*, *Francis of Assisi*, vol. 1, p. 124.
8. Armstrong *et al.*, *Francis of Assisi*, vol. 1, pp. 201–2.
9. 'Third Consideration on the Sacred Stigmata', in Habig, *Omnibus of Sources*, p. 1448.
10. Alphonso, *The Personal Vocation*, p. 14.
11. Armstrong *et al.*, *Francis of Assisi*, vol. 2, p. 542.
12. *The Divine Office*, p. 92*.
13. 'The Second Letter of St Clare to Agnes of Prague', in *Clare of Assisi*, p. 42.
14. 'The Third Letter of St Clare to Agnes of Prague', in *Clare of Assisi*, p. 44.
15. 'The Later Admonition and Exhortation', in Armstrong *et al.*, *Francis of Assisi*, vol. 1, p. 49.
16. Alphonso, *The Personal Vocation*, p. 41

17. Pontifical Work, *In Verbo Tuo*, p. 11.
18. Ibid., p. 18.
19. Cf. Alphonso, *The Personal Vocation*, p. 33.
20. Ibid., p. 32.
21. Pontifical Work, *In Verbo Tuo*, p. 34.
22. Ibid., p. 18.
23. Armstrong *et al.*, *Francis of Assisi*, vol. 1, pp. 124–7.
24. Merrill, *Psalms For Praying*, pp. 279–99; 132–3.
25. 'Later Exhortation (Second Letter to the Faithful)', in Armstrong *et al.*, *Francis of Assisi*, vol. 1, pp. 49–50.

Conclusion

A SPIRITUALITY OF THE HEART is one response to the hunger within the depths of people who seek meaning, purpose and wholeness in the human situation in which they find themselves. It is a rediscovery of the interconnectedness and sacredness of the whole of reality. It is the experience of joy in the beauty of being in relationship. It is an ever-deepening entry into the realm of mystery, wonder, freedom and grace in the *hesed* of God in covenant-love. It is the perception of the gifts of life and love, received from God, shared in God, and returning to God. It is the heart's journey into the heart of God.

By choosing the universally understood symbol of the heart as the prism for understanding afresh the Gospel challenge of conversion, healing and wholeness, we have journeyed into the depths of what it means to be a human person having a unique, personal vocation in life. The symbol of the heart has the ability to address not only the beauty and goodness of the human person, but also the tensions and paradoxes that often exist between being and doing and between union and separateness.

In discovering anew the depth and richness of the human journey we have focused mainly on the revealed Word of God in Scripture and in the Word made flesh, Jesus Christ. In following the footprints of Jesus Christ, the challenge to accept the gift of life and relationships in the raw material and earthiness of our broken humanity, has been centred in the heart, the seat of consciousness.

In Scripture and the Franciscan tradition, the desert, real or symbolic, has been presented as one of the most likely places where the challenge is accepted, confronted and resolved. There, the heart is exposed to the positive and negative aspects that integrates or disintegrates a person on the road to maturity in Christ. Engaging in the struggle within the heart highlights not only the Gospel-centred, incarnational basis of Franciscan spirituality but also the eremitical aspect of our legacy from St Francis. The formative dimension of the desert experience in changing a heart of stone into a heart of flesh, is rooted in the ordinariness of daily life and relationships, applicable to every person, and often seen most clearly and understood most deeply, in the time and place set apart for solitude. For this reason, we invite you, the reader, to experience the invitation of Jesus to 'Come apart and rest for a while' (Mk. 6:31).

Bibliography

Achard of Saint Victor, *Works*, Cistercian Studies Series, 165, translation and Introduction by Hugh Feiss, OSB. Kalamazoo, MI: Cistercian Publications, 2001.

Alphonso, Herbert, SJ, *The Personal Vocation. Transformation in Depth through the Spiritual Exercises*, Rome: Centrum Ignatianum Spiritualitis, 1990.

Armstrong, Regis J., OFM Cap. (ed.), *Clare of Assisi. Early Documents*, New York: Paulist Press, 1988.

Armstrong, Regis J., OFM Cap.; Hellmann, Wayne J.A., OFM, Conv.; Short, William J., OFM, *Francis of Assisi. The Saint. Early Documents*, vol. 1, London: New City Press, 2000.

Armstrong, Regis J., OFM Cap.; Hellmann, Wayne J.A., OFM Conv.; Short, William J., OFM, *Francis of Assisi. The Founder. Early Documents*, vol. 2. London: New City Press, 2000.

Armstrong, Regis J., OFM Cap.; Hellmann, Wayne J.A., OFM, Conv.; Short William J., OFM, *Francis of Assisi. The Prophet. Early Documents*, vol. 3, London: New City Press, 2001.

Armstrong, Regis J., OFM Cap., *St. Francis of Assisi: Writings for a Gospel Life*, USA: St. Paul Publications, 1994.

Augustine, Saint, *The Works of Saint Augustine* (11 volumes), vol. 1: *The Confessions*, edited by John E. Rotelle, OSA, New York: New City Press, 1990–1993.

Augustine, Saint, *The Works of Saint Augustine* (11 volumes), *Sermons,* edited by John E. Rotelle, OSA, New York: New City Press, 1990–1993.

Augustine, Saint, *Tractates on St. John's Gospel*: www.newadvent.org/fathers (date of access: 12 April 2002).

Bonaventure, Saint, *Collationes in Hexaemeron (The Six Days of Creation)*, USA: St. Anthony Guild Press, 1970.

Cassian, John, *The Conferences,* translated and annotated by Boniface Ramsey, *Ancient Christian Writers*, 57, New York: Paulist Press, 1997.

Catechism of the Catholic Church, London: Geoffrey Chapman, 1994.

Delio, I., OSF, *Simply Bonaventure. An Introduction to His Life, Thought, and Writings,* New York: New City Press, 2001.

Divine Office. The Liturgy of the Hours according to the Roman Rite, vol. 1, London: Collins, 1974.

Ephrem, Saint, *Hymns on the Nativity:* www.newadvent.org/fathers (date of access: 12 April 2002).

Foley, Leonard, OFM; Weigel, Jovian, OFM; Normile, Patti, SFO, *To Live as Francis Lived. A Guide for Secular Franciscans*, Cincinnati, OH: St. Anthony Messenger Press, 2000.

Fox, Matthew, *A Spirituality Named Compassion and the Healing of the Global Village. Humpty Dumpty and Us*, USA: Winston Press, 1979.

Frances Teresa, OSC, *Living the Incarnation. Praying with Francis and Clare of Assisi*, London: Darton, Longman & Todd, 1993.

Habig, Marion A. (ed.), *Saint Francis of Assisi, Writings and Early Biographies. English Omnibus of the Sources for the Life of St. Francis*, USA: Franciscan Herald Press, 1983.

Hammond, J.M. (ed.), *Francis of Assisi, History, Hagiography and Hermeneutics in the Early Documents*, New York and London: New City Press, 2004.

Herbert, George, *The Complete Works*, edited by Ann Pasternak Slater, London: David Campbell Publishers, 1994.

Hopkins, Gerard Manley, *Poems and Prose of Gerard Manley Hopkins*, edited by W.H. Gardner, UK & USA: Penguin Books, 1963.

John Paul II, Pope, *Redemptoris Hominis*, Rome: The Vatican, 1979.

Keating, Thomas, *Foundations for Centering Prayer and the Christian Contemplative Life*, New York: The Continuum International Publishing Group, 2002.

Luckman, Harriet A. and Kulzer, Linda, *Purity of Heart in Early Ascetic and Monastic Literature*, Collegeville, MN: The Liturgical Press, 1999.

Matura, Thaddee, OFM, *Francis of Assisi. The Message and His Writings,* translated by Paul Barratt, OFM, NY: Franciscan Institute Publications, St. Bonaventure University, 1997.

Matura, Thaddee OFM, 'My Holy Father' in *Greyfriars Review,* vol. 1, no. 1, NY: The Franciscan Institute, St. Bonaventure University, 1987.

May, Gerald G., *Will and Spirit. A Contemplative Psychology,* San Francisco: Harper & Row, 1982.

Merrill, Nan, *Psalms For Praying: An Invitation to Wholeness,* New York: The Continuum International Publishing Group, 1999.

Metz, Johannes, *Poverty of Spirit,* New York: Newman Press, 1968.

Muto, Susan Annette, *Blessings That Make Us Be. A Formative Approach to Living the Beatitudes,* USA: St. Paul Publications, 1982.

New Jerusalem Bible, London: Darton, Longman & Todd, 1994.

Nouwen, Henri J.M, *The Way of the Heart,* London: Darton, Longman & Todd, 1981.

Origen, *Homelies sur Josue. Sources Chretiennes,* 71, collection edited by H. de Lubac, SJ and J. Danielou, Paris: Les Editions du Cerf, 1960.

Pontifical Work for Ecclesiastical Vocations, *In Verbo Tuo,* Rome: The Vatican, 1997.

Rahner, Karl, 'Heart', *Theological Investigations,* vol. 3, London: Darton, Longman & Todd, 1967.

Raischl, Josef, SFO and Cirino, Andre, OFM (eds), *My Heart's Quest. Collected Writings of Eric Doyle, Friar Minor, Theologian,* England: Franciscan International Study Centre, 2005.

Rohr, Richard, *Job and the Mystery of Suffering. Spiritual Reflections,* New York: Crossroad Publishing Company, 2000.

Squire, Aelred, *Asking the Fathers,* London: SPCK, 1973.

Van Kaam, Adrian, *The Formation of the Human Heart. Formative Spirituality,* vol. 3, New York: Crossroad, 1986.